Succeed in Your Medical School Interview

Stand out from the crowd and get into your chosen medical school

Dr Christopher See

Second edition

KoganPage

LONDON PHILADELPHIA NEW DELHI

First published in Great Britain and the United States in 2011 by Kogan Page Limited
Second edition 2015

2nd Floor, 45 Gee Street
London EC1V 3RS
United Kingdom
www.koganpage.com

1518 Walnut Street, Suite 1100
Philadelphia PA 19102
USA

4737/23 Ansari Road
Daryaganj
New Delhi 110002
India

© Dr Christopher See, 2011, 2015

The right of Dr Christopher See to be identified as the author of this work has been asserted by him in accordance with the Copyright, Designs and Patents Act 1988.

ISBN   978 0 7494 7189 7
E-ISBN   978 0 7494 7190 3

British Library Cataloguing-in-Publication Data

A CIP record for this book is available from the British Library.

Library of Congress Cataloging-in-Publication Data

See, Christopher.
    Succeed in your medical school interview : stand out from the crowd and get into your chosen medical school / Christopher See. – Second edition.
        pages cm
    ISBN 978-0-7494-7189-7 (paperback) – ISBN 978-0-7494-7190-3 (e-ISBN)   1. Medical college applicants–Great Britain.   2. Medical colleges–Great Britain–Admission.   3. Interviewing–Great Britain.   4. Medicine–Vocational guidance–Great Britain.   I. Title.
    R838.4.S443 2015
    610.71'141–dc23

                                                                                2014047407

Typeset by Graphicraft Limited, Hong Kong
Print production managed by Jellyfish
Printed and bound by CPI Group (UK) Ltd, Croydon CR0 4YY

Succeed In Your Medical Sc Int

Contents

Free podcasts of mock interviews can be found on the Kogan Page website.

These can be accessed at **www.koganpage.com/succeed**

Introduction

The interview

The most daunting of the hurdles you need to leap to gain entry to medical school is the interview. By this time, the struggles with examinations, both AS level and specific papers such as the UKCAT and BMAT, will be behind you. The weeks spent crafting a personal statement that best encapsulates you as a potential doctor will be over, and you will be given a moment in the spotlight to convince a panel of doctors that you are indeed the one they wish to select to embark on the long course.

The most heinous crime a teacher, parent or peer advisor can commit is telling candidates that they cannot prepare for interview. Unfortunately, it remains a common urban myth. There are many reasons why people think one cannot prepare for interview: first, that people do not always understand what the interviewer is looking for in a candidate, and second, even if they do have some knowledge of it, they don't have a firm understanding of how to develop the knowledge and skills required to express these qualities to the interview panel.

I hope to dispel that illusion by taking you on a journey in which you will completely prepare for each aspect of the medical school interview in turn. The preparation is not a quick fix, consisting of a few pointers that will magically turn you into a perfect candidate. The knowledge and techniques you will learn and the exercises you will undertake will develop your skills as a communicator, listener, scientist and story-teller. They will help you to build confidence, organize your answers and capture the interest of listeners in a manner that will be useful.

One characteristic I cannot directly teach is interest in medicine. This is something that you will become more and more sure of yourself by reading; going on work experience; and discussing your interest with peers, doctors, medical students, teachers and parents. Many students find that after they explore the career of medicine, it is in fact not for them. Others find that the more they learn about it, the more they wish to know.

One of the things to note is that admissions tutors themselves admit that the procedure is not perfect. Although the task of preparing for interview seems daunting, take some comfort in the fact that each year the majority of candidates will not prepare for interviews in the same diligent way as you are about to. Not only will you need to put in the effort, but you will also need to prepare intelligently. Other students will prepare formulaic answers rather than using key principles and theory to create flexible answers for the endless variants of possible questions. They will not have learned, and then practised, storytelling techniques that will capture the interest of their audience and ultimately make them more memorable. They will have no idea of what to do when faced with seemingly impossible questions on experimental design, data interpretation or scientific analysis. Rest assured that preparation makes a phenomenal difference to interview performance on the day. In a field where competition is at one of the highest levels, you can stand out from the crowd.

In my work as a medical school application tutor, I have seen many students turn from shy, disorganized and frankly knowledge-deficient candidates into keen, confident, mature and structurally brilliant applicants. I use a video analysis technique primarily as an aid to students, not only to be instructed on specific points, but with the aim that they develop the instinct and initiative to correct themselves. You will be able to see some of the results of these candidates, and some of their ingenious, innovative and unusual answers that won them a place at a top medical school of their choice in the UK. I am a practising doctor and teacher of anatomy and I enjoy helping the next generation of doctors prepare themselves for years of training and an exciting career ahead. I look forward to developments in the field and genuinely find my day-to-day work on the wards immensely rewarding. I hope to impart this passion to you, and that you enjoy, as much as humanly possible, this journey into the field of medicine that will form your interview preparation.

How to use this book

The Introduction discusses the interview itself, what to expect and the practical measures you can take to optimize your performance on the day. Chapter 1 looks at the different methods of preparation, separating input procedures such as reading or work experience placements, from output activities such as public speaking, mock interviews and other specialist learning exercises. Chapter 2 presents the somewhat mysterious interview process as an understandable model, known as chain theory, and describes how to manage the macro elements of the interview and manipulate the flow of questions. Motivation for medicine, which forms the initial and sometimes most challenging part of the interview is discussed in Chapter 3. This chapter illustrates how to avoid being uninteresting by using a storytelling technique known as dinner party theory (DPT). Chapter 4 looks at a new interview method that is growing in popularity: the Multiple Mini-Interview (MMI) and how do deal with its unique series of challenges. Work experience and voluntary work questions are analysed in Chapter 5, along with the importance of keeping a work experience diary.

Chapter 6 gives information on how to answer demanding personal attribute questions about teamwork, leadership, communication skills and many others. Questions surrounding the medical school itself are addressed in Chapter 7. Chapter 8 deals with the issues involved in medicine as a profession, and how good a grasp you as a potential future doctor have on them. Chapter 9 looks at knowledge of hospital life and the NHS. Chapter 10 tackles the vast amount of medically-related knowledge that will be useful in your interview, and how to organize your answers on the science of medicine.

In Chapter 11 there are examples of ethical and legal dilemmas that are often posed to interviewees, and a mechanism for systematic analysis known as the four principles approach is explained. Chapter 12 is specifically for international students applying to UK medical schools. Chapter 13 deals with questions for the particularly competitive graduate entry courses for graduate students. The unique, arduous and exciting experience that is the Oxbridge interview is explored in Chapter 14, which gives a number of worked examples of how to answer the most difficult of questions. Candidates can make use of the methods and frameworks contained within to synthesize excellent responses to questions, even if they do not know the answer.

Learning tasks

Much of the value of reading this book will be learning from the experiences of others, accelerating your own performance by not having to stumble through the mistakes yourselves. However, there are some elements of preparing for interview that require human interaction and there are recommended activities in the 'learning task' sections. Some of them you will be able to undertake in your work experience, others with your peers, teachers or others. They are activities that you might not otherwise think to do, but will practise an element of communication in a manner not normally covered by simple reading and one or two mock interviews, which is the staple of most students.

Example answers and case studies

Reading the examples of other students, and seeing what they have done well or badly, will be of great help in your pursuit of a place at medical school. You will be able to see what kind of techniques successful students employed, and also some of the more amusing stories of what goes wrong in an interview. Bear in mind that people who make mistakes, slip-ups and attempts at humour do still make it to medical school, and one positive thing to take from reading their stories is that it is difficult to scupper an interview with a single error. Do not be put off or focus on a single mistake as you will be able to turn the tide of the interview in your favour again with a solid overall performance.

The interview process

Even before you have received your instructions for attending your interview, you should begin to prepare carefully. The background knowledge and reading, learning tasks and practising of verbal and non-verbal skills will require several months of hard work. The areas of knowledge that you will need to draw upon in your answers can be organized by the types of questions, which are in turn reflected by the chapters of this book.

The interview itself varies to some degree from university to university, but there are some common elements. You will almost certainly be interviewed by more than one person. There may be multiple interviews, which are usually split roughly into 'academic' and 'personal' types. However, preparing with this book will allow you to address either of these individually, or together, by identifying the type of questions and formulating your answers accordingly.

The interview panel

- The panel will consist of at least one practising doctor.
- There may be members of staff from the faculty who will go on to be your teachers at university.
- There may also be a current medical student, who will offer an opinion to the panel and may ask you questions.
- There may be a lay, non-medical person on the panel.

Oxbridge interviews

Oxbridge interviews are so different from other medical school interviews in terms of content, aim and admissions criteria that they can be considered a totally different process altogether. You will be interviewed at your college of choice, and possibly by another college as well. Interviews tend to take place earlier than those for other universities, and may commence from the beginning of December. The types of questions, and the type of candidate these universities are looking for, are detailed in Chapter 14.

The night before the interview

Logistics

If you are applying to a university in another city, you will probably be staying over-night. Make sure you have left enough time for travel between locations.

Avoid learning new material

You will have covered a vast amount of material in your preparations up to this point and the most useful thing you can do now is to consolidate what you already know. Information will either be 'interview ready' – which is to say data that you know well, and more than just the bare bones – or not. Moreover, it is important that you are comfortable in verbalizing and discussing the material, and this comes about by a combination of input (reading and research) as well as practising output (in mock interviews, practice with friends or talking about it in front of a mirror). Any new information you acquire in the last couple of days before your interview will not be retained at such a high quality and therefore you should not attempt to cram in new data. Remember that, having read this book, you will be able to use chain navigation and cadences to steer the interview away from unfamiliar topics, but also remember that you should be equipped with a method of dealing with the unknown. Nevertheless, it is a common mistake of medical students to be reading some new article or book on the night before – avoid following in their footsteps.

Relaxation

It is very important that your mind is fresh and enthusiastic for the challenge ahead. Just as an actor who practises a scene too many times might find it hard to look surprised when a murderer appears from around the curtain for the 30th time, you might lose the will to discuss your love of science if it has been going through your head too often the night before the examination. You will therefore need an activity that can genuinely take your mind off things for a short period when you need a break. Some students take music, a non-medical book, a film or TV series to relax with, others like to talk to friends on the phone or surf the internet. Whatever your choice, make sure you can take your mind away from the task the next day and refresh yourself.

Revision materials

Construct revision sheets to refresh yourself on key definitions and terms; also write down the anecdotes that you can draw upon for questions on medicine, personal attributes and work experience.

Nutrition

Experiment with your meals, and find the type of food that you can eat without it making you feel sleepy – try to have the same or similar products available for the day of interview itself so you will be able to perform at your best. For many people, fat-rich foods such as fish and chips cause bloating and wind, which you may be keen to avoid. Sugary foods often give a 'high' as blood glucose levels peak, but then give a rebound 'low' as increasing insulin levels drive the glucose into the cells, leaving you feeling shaky and weak. Caffeine can lead to an over-aroused state in which you may answer too quickly or without sufficient thought and it may also heighten feelings of anxiety.

However, all of the above are just guidelines. The point is that people respond variably to different foods and it is important to establish your own personal optimal nutrition in the pre-interview period. You may also find these data useful around examination periods. It would be a shame for a future doctor to give a poor performance because of lack of knowledge of nutritional metabolism, both theoretical and applied!

On the morning of the interview

When you wake up, just remember that if you've been working through the exercises, questions and learning tasks in this book, you will be better prepared than most candidates. Be reassured that there are many people who think that one cannot prepare for interview, and you will be in a good position. The last thing to remember is that you are applying for a long course at university and working life after that, and that you should be genuinely looking forward to it, as a wonderful, rich and exciting experience, culminating in a challenging and rewarding career.

In the interview itself

Managing the questions and answers themselves is the subject of most of the book. However, there are several practical points to be aware of for the interview itself.

Anxiety management

Remember that every student will be anxious, and the interviewers expect this and will not count it against you, so long as you are not a nervous wreck and cannot give any answers. Almost all students find that once the first few questions are out of the way, they get into the flow of things and relax into a more natural tone.

Body language

There are certain body positions that give the impression of negativity and should be avoided, such as crossing your arms or legs, or leaning or slouching back into your chair. Try to avoid irritating mannerisms such as flicking hair, crunching knuckles or tapping. These can be picked up in mock interviews by your interviewer's feedback, or seen on video.

However, do not focus too heavily on your body language once inside the interview. From video analysis of many candidates, I have noted that you will look confident if you are well prepared and your answers are organized, interesting and insightful, even if you happen to cross your legs or arms when you are sitting. You will not appear confident if you assume a legs-uncrossed, forwards-leaning body position, but are poorly prepared and anxious about what to say. It is important to find a sitting position that suits you and allows you to speak up.

Listening

Focus on listening to the words and content of the question, rather than trying to look like an active listener. Some students can get so focused on non-verbal techniques such as nodding and saying 'mm' as the interviewer speaks that they lose concentration on the material the question is asking for.

Attitude

- Be enthusiastic. Admissions tutors will want to see a genuine interest in medicine and also a genuine determination to win a place at their medical school. Be prepared to give a high-energy, intelligent performance and try to enjoy discussing the topics with the interviewers as much as possible.

- Be humble. Several interviewers have said that one of the biggest turn-offs for interviewers, and one problem that occurs year upon year, is the arrogant candidate. As a future medical student, remember that you are still young in the eyes of the panel and that they are looking for your potential to learn, not necessarily how much you have actually learned so far. Having a good attitude towards taking on board criticism and accepting when you do not know something is an important part of being a medical student and a doctor, and you should demonstrate this in the interview by engaging in reasoned promotion of yourself, and learning from the input of the panel as you go along.

- Be polite. Shake hands firmly if prompted to by the panel members, and remember to thank them at the end of the proceedings.

Dress code

The dress code for interview is formal. For men, this means suit and tie in conservative colours, smart and polished shoes, tidy appearance and no unnatural hair colours. For women it means a suit or skirt suit in similarly conservative hues with moderate make-up and accessories. This is not specified by all universities, but when applying for a course that leads to professional career, it helps the admissions tutor to extrapolate how you might choose to present yourself in the future.

After the interview

It can be helpful to confer with fellow interviewees about how they found the experience, what questions and answers they gave. However, be careful not to dwell on the negatives, or get too down if another candidate gave a 'perfect answer' to a particular question; the interview is scored as a whole and not too much weight is given to any individual question. You can reflect on your own performance if you have other interviews to come and this may reveal where you need to improve in terms of knowledge, understanding or communication. Make sure you take some time to unwind after the stressful experience.

Summary

- Ensure that your logistics are in order for the night before your interview.
- Do some active relaxation to take your mind off the interview.
- Get a good night's sleep.
- Eat well and correctly.
- Remember and apply the basic principles of DPT and chain navigation.
- Try not to focus too hard on body language once you are inside the interview – let it come naturally.
- Look forward to your future in medicine, and be genuinely excited!

CHAPTER 1

Preparation for the interview

Preparation for the interview involves two discrete stages, the first being the input of the vast amounts of knowledge you will require. This stage is necessary but not sufficient for an exceptional performance at interview. The second is the processing and output of the information you have acquired, in a fluent, intellectual and analytical manner that will greatly increase your chances of gaining the favour of the admissions tutors and thereby your place in medical school.

This chapter will detail how to maximize your input by use of both reading and experience. It will also explore the avenues available to practise, by use of mock interviews, other public speaking exercises and some methods to improve your linguistic dexterity.

Input

Extra-curricular reading can form an important part of your preparation, helping you to answer a variety of NHS, medicine and science questions comfortably. Keeping up with current affairs will be helpful in demonstrating your interest in modern medicine and involves continuous learning and development.

Basic level

At a basic level, you will be reading about science and medicine in the news, such as on the BBC news health and science website or in any broadsheet newspaper.

Intermediate level

Intermediate-level reading includes scientific and medical journals, such as the *Student British Medical Journal* (*sBMJ*) and *New Scientist*.

Advanced level

At advanced level, you will read industry-standard peer-reviewed journals, such as:

- *Nature*;

- the *New England Journal of Medicine* (*NEJM*);

- the *Lancet*;

- the *British Medical Journal* (*BMJ*).

Non-medical reading

This may include:

- the *Economist*;

- broadsheet newspapers;

- popular science books.

There are several steps to maximize your gains from reading. First, ensure that you keep a copy of each article for future reference. Next, try to write a three-sentence summary of each article. This will be useful as you will need to express the main point of the article to the interview panel swiftly, with enough detail to begin discussing it. You can note elements of your current knowledge that tie into the subject, for example if you read an article about the mechanisms of harm in smoking, you might write down some key points about respiration that you learned from biology and that might be useful in answering an interview question. Last, you can do further reading around the topic at hand, which will enable you to speak more comfortably and in depth if probed by the interview panel. Taking the above example, you could read up on lung cancer, the history of smoking and its role in heart disease.

> Keep the copies of the articles you have read along with your notes in a folder that you can return to when you are preparing for your interview. You can organize the material by topic, date or question type.

Experiences such as voluntary work and work experience placements are discussed in detail in Chapter 4.

Output

This is the final goal of preparation, as the information you have stored must be processed and expressed in order for it to have any value. This element of the training is the one most neglected by students in terms of preparation. It is true that without diligent effort on the input front, very little will be achieved by practising output. However, if your reading, research and experiences are solid, you will need to learn how to maximize your use of them. There are several methods you can use, as listed below.

Mock interviews

These can be done at school, undertaken by private companies or with peers, teachers, parents or even friends. It is difficult to simulate accurately the pressure of speaking to a stranger, let alone a panel of strangers, in a formal setting, and if your interview is your first experience of this you may expect to find it unnerving and to use a considerable amount of your attention adapting to these foreign feelings and experience. However, if you have some familiarity with the process, you can concentrate on the task at hand, which is to show that you have the qualities necessary to become a doctor by expressing them in your answers to the panel.

Learning tasks

The second method is to use learning tasks that train you for particular aspects of the interview process. For example, for dinner party theory (DPT) training (see Chapter 3), you may be undertaking tasks at social events, parties or at school. Read the learning tasks given in some chapters, as these will help you prepare in unusual ways that will challenge and stimulate you.

Acting, debating and public speaking

I would positively encourage students to try and participate in activities that require vocal expression, processing of information and conquering anxiety. As a student participating in the model UN, I remember being frozen in fear as I had to make my first points. However, as with any process, this fear faded away. I also learned a great deal from watching and listening to others and, in particular, what kind of proposals I found interesting and compelling, and which ones were poor and unconvincing. Learning to synthesize arguments on the spot and using the information you have in an applied fashion are skills you can learn in debating and answering questions in public speaking.

Acting is also a good way to build confidence in a slightly different manner, as it takes a good deal of courage to face a packed audience on opening night. There is nothing to stop you from standing there mute with fear, other than the will to speak up and be heard. It is training this will and desire to communicate in the face of fear and pressure that will be valuable to you in the interview process.

However, not everyone will enjoy such activities, nor will everyone be suited to them. There are infinite opportunities to learn about the output element of communication, from listening to a dedicated rugby captain giving the pre-match team talk, organizing an event and learning how to structure your instructions to your subordinates, to planning strategy under the gaze of spectators in the finals of the school chess tournament. Whatever you choose to do, practising under pressure, and learning what works and what does not from observing others around you, will serve you well.

Oxbridge

Preparing for Oxbridge is yet another story (see Chapter 14). First, you must be comfortable with the differences between other medical schools and Oxbridge, and this will come from reading, research and talking to past and current students. You will also benefit from a wide range of reading, including literature and current affairs as well as other disciplines such as history, art, physics and economics. However, the focus will always be scientific ability and interest, and you should focus your attention on learning how to put your scientific knowledge to good use. School science societies, presentations, laboratory work experiences, scientific reading and discussion can all help in this pursuit.

The Scrubs, House MD or ER game

This can be a fun way to work on medical enunciation with friends. Watch an episode of your favourite medical drama. Every time one of the actors says a medical word you don't know, you have to repeat it after the actor. You'll be shouting 'haematoma' and 'haemodynamically stable' at the TV screen in no time at all. However, the person who is the consistently the slowest has to go and look up what the condition is and explain a bit about it to the group the following week.

As the more astute of you will have noticed, this is a little bit similar to how a problem-based learning (PBL) session might work, and is also a light-hearted way to keep up with medical knowledge. It also aids the output aspect of medical speaking, not only in the game, but also for the person who has to explain the condition next week. Getting into the habit of describing diseases and treatments to a peer group will help your confidence and preparation.

Summary

- Both input and output are important in the interview process.

- Input involves both reading and experience.

- Extra-curricular reading can be guided.

- Non-medical reading can be particularly helpful for Oxbridge interviews.

- Output preparation helps produce a polished final product in interview.

- Mock interviews are the closest practice for actual interviews, if they are undertaken well by student and examiner.

- Acting, public speaking and debating can help develop skills in confidence and delivery.

- Medical games are a good way to enlarge your medical vocabulary painlessly.

CHAPTER 2

Interview macro-analysis – chain theory

Chain theory

There are three main processes that guide the course of an interview. They can be characterized as follows:

- continuous chain (c-chain) questions;

- antagonistic chain (a-chains) questions;

- pedantic comments or questions (p-stops).

Admissions tutors admit that apart from glaringly horrific or dangerous answers, individual answers will not determine the outcome of an interview. The most important impression is in consistently providing well-structured, thought-out and interesting answers. Several tutors have described the best candidates as having a 'natural flow' to the conversation, and the pattern of question and answer. Therefore, we must understand how this flow develops, and how we can anticipate and prepare for a flow. Scientific-type questions follow a slightly different pattern, which is covered in Chapter 14, as they require a different skill set to navigate.

Continuous chain questions

The majority of your interview questions will be of a continuous chain (c-chain) variety. This involves the initial question, which can be on any topic, and based on your answer, admissions tutors use this as a tool to explore your insight and knowledge.

C-chain questions include 'Why do you want to study medicine?' The answer could include your interest in science, the humanitarian side and work experience. This initial question is the root of the chain of questioning, and is called the c-stem. The c-chain would then be propagated down the path of either:

- your interest in science – for example 'You mentioned biology, are there any particular areas in biology you enjoyed studying?' or 'Why is chemistry important in medicine?';

- your humanitarian side – for example 'You mentioned you have done some voluntary work, what kind of activities did you undertake and why did you find them valuable?'; or

- your work experience – for example 'Tell me about what you learned from your work experience.'

There are some tools you can use to steer the conversation down one of the c-paths to keep the interview on your preferred topics. Remember that maintaining interest is an overriding 'macro' goal of the interview and influencing the direction of the c-path can keep you away from topics that you are less comfortable in establishing interesting conversation about.

Cadence

This a method by which you can use the structure and tone of your reply to signal the most interesting c-path. In a multi-part answer, the follow-on question is most likely to be about the last answer, followed by the beginning answer, and least likely to be concerned with the middle. For example, the answer might be 'My interest in medicine comes from a combination of a love of sciences and a genuine desire to help people, which I have discovered more about through volunteer work.'

Just as in physics, current flows down the path of least resistance, so an interviewer will usually follow the c-path of most interest. The interviewer will pick up on the cue of voluntary work and ask you about what you learned from that. However, it is important that you do not try to anticipate the next question. Rather, use the above techniques to help the conversation spend a majority of the time on subjects in which you feel more comfortable. In the worked example above, you should feel comfortable talking about both sciences and volunteer work.

Interviewers may want to explore areas that you have glossed over to see if you are hiding a gap in your knowledge or understanding. Therefore, it is important that when you are using c-chain manipulation you are ready for questions you are not expecting.

Antagonistic chain questions

As the interview progresses, you may encounter a question chain that starts with a relatively neutral question then takes a turn down a more confrontational route. This is an antagonistic chain or a-chain. One of the common patterns of questioning behaviour might be something similar to the following.

Candidate: 'I want to study medicine because I want to help people in a direct manner.'
Interviewer: 'If you want to really help people in a hands-on way, why don't you become a nurse?'
or
Candidate: 'I really want to work for an international aid organization such as MSF.'
Interviewer: 'I see, and do you think the government should fund the training for doctors who want to go off and work in foreign countries?'

The a-chain centres around the interviewer challenging the interview by directly opposing the candidate's point of view, and seeing how he or she responds. Unlike the p-stop (described later), an a-chain is more of a diagnostic tool and will commonly feature in the interviews of candidates who are performing well. Admissions tutors are looking for the following qualities by using a-chains:

● performance under pressure;

●, reasoned argument;

● ability to maintain emotional distance from responses;

● ability to assimilate new information and learn from it.

Navigating an a-chain

Your goal is to demonstrate fully to the interviewer the qualities listed above. Poor responses are fast, unipolar and defensive answers. You can use the following framework for terminating an a-chain and bringing the questioning back to c-chains.
   The **a-chain navigation framework** consists of:

1 thinking pause;

2 acknowledgement;

3 arguments for;

4 arguments against;

5 balanced conclusion.

Each phase is explained in detail below, along with worked examples.

Thinking pause

It is important to take a little extra time to consider an a-chain response, more so than other questions, first because you will probably need the time to balance both sides of the argument. Second, if you are a candidate who has a tendency to rush out answers, this will look especially bad in a-chain responses as the interviewers are looking for reasoned answers rather than knowledge recall.

Acknowledgement

Acknowledge the interviewers' position. Interviewers are looking to see if you are aware that their statement is controversial. Demonstrate your awareness of the complexity of the problem they are proposing. For example; in response to the a-chain question, 'If you want to really help people in a hands on way, why don't you become a nurse?', you would acknowledge this by using a statement such as, 'Actually nursing has quite a lot of similarities with what I would like to achieve.'

Arguments for and against

Advance arguments for both sides, in a neutral manner, using phrases such as 'some people believe' or 'on the one hand'. Present the arguments in the third person rather than expressing what you think, for example, 'Euthanasia can be considered a good thing if it eases the suffering of patients' rather than 'I think euthanasia helps to ease the suffering of patients.' This helps to maintain your impartiality at this stage.

Balanced conclusion

Use verbal triggers to indicate to the interviewers that you are concluding your argument. These are not catchphrases to score points, but signposts that you are reaching the end of the answer, such as: 'on balance', 'with these things in mind' and 'taking these into consideration'.

Associating value to arguments can help in demonstrating the intellectual process of balancing. For example, in answer to the nursing question above, you could say that you value scientific interest and compassion equally and therefore you are choosing medicine because it has a similar amount of compassion but more focus on science. This is a semi-quantitative balancing that demonstrates good reason. Simply saying 'on balance' does not necessarily show you have performed an analysis in this way.

Here is an example of a-chain navigation.

Interviewer's question: 'Why should we pick you rather than other, better qualified candidates?'

This is how not to answer: 'Are you sure they are all better qualified than me?' (This is a real answer from a mock interview.)

Here is how to answer:

'I would say that the qualifications required for medicine include academic ones, as well as those regarding teamwork, leadership, communication skills, empathy and dedication. Therefore, I do appreciate that there will be candidates who are better qualified in all of these fields than me, and others who are better qualified in some but not all of them. On the other hand, I also believe that I have worked hard to become a rounded academic and compassionate candidate, and therefore I hope I am better qualified than some others as well. Taking into consideration the candidates who are better qualified than me on paper, I think there are some intangible qualities that I will bring to the course that are harder to measure, and the most significant of these is my interest and desire to study medicine. This is not a formal qualification, but something that I can only express in my words and actions up until now. Therefore, I sincerely hope you will pick me, and I hope to demonstrate that this desire to study medicine will help make me an excellent medical student and future doctor, even in the face of my strong competition.'

Have a sense of humour. This can help to mitigate over-seriousness. Make sure that your humour is appropriate and not too coarse or offensive.

Know your limits. It is much better to say that you don't know something than to be caught out not knowing something. This also reflects on your future practice for medicine where it is vitally important to know where the limits of your knowledge lie.

Be friendly. An interview is really a conversation about yourself and reflects how you might speak to patients or people in general.

Be up to date on current affairs and have a considered opinion on them.

An a-chain will be progressive and challenging. You will have the opportunity to defend your position, and if you response is well-considered, it is within reason the a-chain will be terminated and questioning will move back to c-chains.

Pedantic comments or questions

Interview candidates have often been faced with the following kind of situation.

Candidate: 'I have always been interested in medicine.'
Interviewer: 'Always? So, you've not really considered other careers.'
or
Candidate: 'I was so tired I literally died.'
Interviewer: 'I think you mean you figuratively died. If you had literally died, you wouldn't be here.'

These incidences of interruption of the narrative of the candidate with a mundane, or non-helpful and non-progressive comment is known as a pedantic stop or p-stop. It is a tool used by interviewers to break up the flow of a candidate and see how he or she responds to criticism. However, it is also a manifestation of dissatisfaction with the method of delivery of your answers. When interviewers find a candidate imprecise with grammar or, more significantly, with logic or knowledge, they will often indicate this to the candidate by initiating a p-stop.

Prevention

Ideally, the management of p-stops is effective prophylaxis. Use grammatical structures with a degree of academic caution. For example, rather than using words such as 'always' or 'definitely', consider softer options such as 'mostly' and 'commonly'. If, for example, you state 'Leaders always have good verbal communication skills', you might be given counter-examples proving you wrong, such as the silent leader who inspires by example. Introducing elements of humbleness in answers will also help to prevent the manifestation of p-stops.

> You can make use of some academically cautious constructs, such as:
>
> 'From what I have experienced so far...';
>
> 'As far as I am aware...';
>
> 'I am beginning to learn about...';
>
> 'I have read that...';
>
> 'Some people might consider...'.

Interviewers will be responsive to your performance. Several admissions tutors have mentioned that if a candidate has an interesting, balanced and intelligent narrative, they will often try to avoid interrupting. Conversely, they will have no hesitation in interrupting a candidate with poor structure or who is imprecise with language. This is not with malicious intent, but is an attempt to allow the candidate to realize the errors, much like one might defibrillate a heart in ventricular fibrillation in the hope that it will restart in a more rhythmic fashion.

Acute management

If you do come across a p-stop, take it as an opportunity to have a pause and rethink the direction of your answer. First, verbally acknowledge the criticism, apologize and correct yourself. This is important in demonstrating how you deal with critical feedback. It also reflects on how you might perform under similar feedback in a clinical or educational setting.

Do not use phrases such as 'I meant to say...', which is retrospective correction and indicates some resistance to the criticism. Prospective statements such as 'I'm sorry, I should say...' indicate that you accept the error, and look forward to correcting future practice, which is important both in grammar and medicine. For example, you might manage this p-stop in the following manner.

Candidate: 'I have always been interested in medicine.'

Interviewer: 'Always? So, you've not really considered other careers.'

Candidate: 'I'm sorry, I should say I have been interested in medicine for a long time, I suppose it seems a bit like "always" by now, but really it started when I was choosing which GCSEs to take, and I realized that the subject I most enjoyed was biology. I then...'

Minimize the time spent focused on an error by expanding your answer after the prospective correction.

A candidate who receives several p-stops but fails to respond appropriately is likely to score poorly, particularly in the areas of potential to be taught and communication skills. A candidate who receives a p-stop and successfully navigates it, and takes it as a cue to manage his or her language better, will score well.

Ideally, through careful and intelligent expression and discussion of ideas, p-stops should be prevented and this will be one factor that reflects a high-scoring candidate.

Summary

- Interview questions may be divided into several types, which can be identified by key features.

- The successful navigation of question chains requires different techniques, as they are used to assess different attributes.

- C-chain questions test communication skills and knowledge recall.

- A-chain questions test reasoned argument and performance under pressure.

- The path that a question chain follows can be influenced by the candidate using tools such as cadence and structure.

- Prophylaxis of p-stops requires careful use of grammar and academic caution. This can be achieved by practice and preparation of answers.

- Acknowledgement and prospective correction is the best way to navigate p-stops once they occur.

- A high frequency of p-stops is a poor indicator of performance.

CHAPTER 3

Motivation for medicine

Introduction

Open questions, such as 'Why do you want to study medicine?', are the most commonly asked in interviews. They tend to be open in the sense that you can shape the answer however you desire, and this in turn causes great anxiety for students; since there is no fixed structure, students get lost in the infinite possibilities of ways to answer. Answering these questions in order to come across as an excellent potential medical student and future doctor requires the art of becoming a storyteller. Admissions tutors repeatedly state that one of the key selection criteria for students is to have an interesting interview, as this reflects both how genuinely enthused a candidate is, as well as being someone with good human-to-human communication skills. Therefore, it is vital for candidates to learn not only what to answer the questions with, but how.

This chapter describes a method for generating interesting answers based on conversational style with structure, known as dinner party theory (DPT). It also gives details of the types of question you may encounter, with example answers demonstrating key learning points.

How to become a great storyteller – dinner party theory (DPT)

Once you have acquired background knowledge, it is important to consider how you are going to use it to give yourself the best chance of success. DPT is a model I have developed specifically for medical school interviews, which was designed after consultation with admissions tutors from many universities, including Oxbridge, and draws on observations of social successes and failures in interacting with people. If you consider a dinner party, where you sit down next to people you have never met before, what are the factors that make someone interesting to talk to?

Let us consider the following situation.

'Hi, I'm Ricky.'
'Hello, I'm Janine.'
'Nice to meet you. So what do you do?'

Consider the following responses.

'I'm a student.'

This is a simple statement of fact or list. The disadvantage is that Ricky will then have to prompt Janine again to extrapolate more data about what being a student actually involves. This makes the conversation feel like work, and several admissions tutors have stated that they dislike having to drag information and thought out of candidates.

'I'm an English student.'
'I'm studying English literature, focusing on the works of Austen.'
'I'm studying English literature, focusing on the works of Austen and I hope to go on to a career in journalism.'

These responses are increasingly more interesting, and warrant a follow-up question. This adds an element of personal touch, which is information relating to the person as opposed to the activity and therefore individual to this person. In this case it is her aspiration to a career in journalism. This response makes the follow-up questioning far easier as it gives a number of cues to pick up on. It also gives the would-be journalist an advantage too, by directing the conversation to areas that she might be more comfortable talking about. It is also good micro-management, as the answer intrinsically generates interest, and the person asking the question feels curious to find out more. How might we apply these observations to interview questions?

We can model the type of answers in a 'hierarchy of interest', going from the most bland to the most stimulating.

Hierarchy of interest

The hierarchy is:

- list;
- explain;
- link with theory;
- manifest (give an example);
- reflect.

Imagine the question 'Can you tell me about your work experience?' in terms of the hierarchy of interest:

- List – 'I did two weeks at hospital X, three weeks at hospital Y and another one month placement in a lab.' The lowest level of interest is generated by simple reporting. It is an absolute chore to mine further information from this candidate.

- Explain – 'I've done an attachment to a cardiology unit, an orthopaedics ward and spent a month in a biochemistry laboratory.' This is similar to listing, but adds more detail, which adds a degree of interest, and allows the interviewer to picture more of what went on. However, this would still require 'work' on the part of the interviewer to interrogate the candidate about the specific activities, which diminishes interest.

- Link with theory – 'I've done an attachment to a cardiology unit, an orthopaedics ward and spent a month in a biochemistry laboratory. These work experiences have been a good way for me to learn about a career in medicine.' This takes a step further in answering the question by linking the work experiences with the theory behind the question – which is essentially what the candidate knows about medicine, and how serious he or she is. However, while it is informative, it is uninteresting and impersonal.

- Manifest (give an example) – 'I've done an attachment to a cardiology unit where I followed the junior doctors around to see what they do every day. I saw doctors examining patients, listening to their heart and lungs and then correlating the findings by looking at X-rays and ECGs.'

- Reflect on how it made you feel – 'I found this combination of hands-on work and integrating it with intellectual processes really stimulating and rewarding, and I would love to do this in my career in the future.'

    In order to tell a good story, there are many factors required. First, the material. There is a minimum amount of key knowledge that is a prerequisite to answering a question; for example, answering 'Why do you want to become a doctor?' requires a knowledge of what the life of a doctor involves. However, the more you know about it, the richer your answer will potentially be. Most people know that being a doctor involves scientific knowledge and helping others.

DPT is most useful for questions that involve a degree of recounting events from your own life or describing yourself. These are mostly found in the medical and personal questions, although the principles of DPT can be applied to most questions.

Correct use of DPT involves a degree of preparation beyond that undertaken by most candidates for interview. It is important that you consider the potential questions and take time to explore all facets of the answers. For example, in answering the question 'What makes you a good candidate for us?', it is important to consider what you will actually be doing at medical school, as well as what is involved in being a doctor. You could use the knowledge of the subjects taught at medical school to link with your own experiences to answer this question.

A framework for answering questions using DPT is given below.

DPT framework

- Explain the theory.

- Report the event.

- Manifest (give an example).

- Maintain interest with a unique perspective.

- Reflect on how it made you feel.

- Conclude.

Application of DPT

The fundamental principle of DPT is that when you answer a question, you make it interesting, relevant and intelligent. Answers will typically begin with the explanation of the theory, which can include definitions, and will move on to giving examples, maintaining interest and reflecting upon the subject, with a clear-cut conclusion.

The maintaining interest section is the most important part of DPT. Admissions tutors admit that they sometimes get frustrated with the interview process as it produces 'a lot of the same answers from the same questions, which is frightfully dull'. As we established earlier, having an interesting interview is the best correlation with a successful application, so this boredom is exactly what we want to avoid. The question is how to avoid being the 15th person that day to give the same answers.

Let us consider what admissions tutors will already know about work experiences. They will already know that students are most likely to be observing rather than doing anything active. They will not know about the interesting patient you spoke to who had ruptured his cruciate ligament, who you felt most empathy for as it ended his years of playing football. They will not know about the inspiring doctor you met who had a wonderful attitude towards the patients he treated, especially the confused patient with dementia who thought he was in a police station, when he managed to calm him down and lead him back to his bed.

Consider the question 'What is your greatest achievement?' in terms of the DTP framework:

- Explain the theory – 'I feel the most difficult things to achieve are long term.'

- Report the event – 'My karate class offered many opportunities for achievement.'

- Manifest – give an example (fact) – 'I would say my greatest achievement is my black belt in karate. I trained for eight years at school.'

- Maintain interest with a unique perspective (description) – 'It was a gruelling regime having training after a long day at school, and at times it was physically very demanding, such as having bare feet in a wooden gym in the middle of winter! As you can imagine, it was tough going.' (Gestures are used appropriately at this stage.) Maintaining interest is the most important part of effective DPT. It gives a real, personal and unique spin on your answer and will stimulate interest and empathy from your interview panel. Other candidates may give similar theory and manifested results, but you can create a more memorable and lasting impression if you address the admissions tutors with some facts or anecdotes that they will not have heard before.

- Reflect – 'I learned a great deal about discipline and commitment from persevering until I reached my goal of black belt, and I learned that I can apply myself to an activity regularly and consistently. I hope to carry these skills over into my future study of medicine.' Reflective learning is a key element of medical education, and involves considering not only the event that you experienced, but also how it affected you, and how it will change what you do in the future.

- Conclude – 'So, I feel this is my most treasured achievement.' (Candidate gives a slight nod.) The use of body language becomes important here, as the use of your hands, body and expression will help to signal to the interviewers when there is an 'interesting' section of your story. The most critical point is that there should be a change of atmosphere when you are at the segment of the answer that is designed to maintain interest. This is achieved by the combination of content as well as non-verbal communication. You can use words or phrases such as 'on balance', 'overall', or 'finally' to indicate that you have come to the end of your answer. This maintains a smooth transition between question and answer that allows more information exchange in a shorter time, and allows you to score more highly than other candidates, provided that your answers are good ones.

DPT feedback

Just as a good comedian responds to the crowd, you too must be responsive to your audience, the interviewers. There is a time limit in which you have to execute your DPT routine in answer to a question, governed by the fact that interviews are finite events. If you exceed the time that you are allowed for a response, you will receive either direct or indirect cues from the interviewers to wrap up your story and move on. Indirect cues are predominantly given through body language, and some of the possible signs are listed below. A direct cue will be a verbal instruction to move on, and you should ignore one of these at your peril.

Look for:

- eyes glazing over;

- fidgeting;

- reducing eye contact;

- sighing or coughing.

In the early stages of practising DPT, students have found that they either ramble on for too long when giving an answer or are too brief. It is vitally important that you practise your DPT skills on a daily basis in order to gain feedback. This can occur in speaking to peers, teachers, at parties, on the phone, or almost any situation where you are called upon to communicate. You can gauge the responses from your interviewers and readjust the timing and content to improve these responses. Remember that doctors are scientists, and that by trying different formulations of the same information, you might get different results.

Learning tasks

Introduce yourself to some new people at a party and ask them about what they like to do in their spare time. Assess how well their responses use DPT, and answer them back using it. Take heed of any indicators of disinterest.

Find a teacher you do not know particularly well, and ask for 5 minutes of his or her time to discuss your career plans. Explain why you want to study medicine and answer any questions that may arise. Note the teacher's non-verbal feedback, judging it as good or bad. Then go through the same process with another teacher, aiming for improved feedback.

Summary

- The primary aim of DPT is to make the interviewers enjoy the interview and find you interesting as a person. This is a key criteria for selection.

- The DPT framework is most useful for questions about medicine and personal attributes.

- Avoid remaining solely on the theoretical plane for questions about medicine and personal attributes.

- Use anecdotes that are tried and tested to be interesting.

- Always be alert for direct and indirect feedback and respond accordingly.

- Reflect on what you have learned.

- Conclude strongly.

Questions

Open questions

1. Why do you want to study medicine?

This is undoubtedly the most common interview question and should be well antici-pated. In preparing your answer, you can consider the following points:

- Tell your individual **story** of how you first considered medicine as a career.

- Show how you then **developed** this interest and explored the career of medicine through work experience, community service and interest in science.

- You can reference influential figures or experiences, for example your own or a family member's experience in hospital if relevant.

- Medicine is a career of lifelong learning. Demonstrate that you are enthusiastic, yet realize that you still have a lot to learn about this career, rather than trying to show that you know it all.

- Your personal statement will no doubt contain some elements of this answer. You can cover some of the same ground, but try to expand on your statement where possible.

Example answer

'As I progressed through school I found myself swinging towards the sciences as my main interest. I was probably most influenced by a biology teacher in year 10 who I thought was fantastic, and really made me think about science and how it applied to our everyday lives. With that in mind, when I started to think of what to do with my future, I felt that medicine was a perfect reflection of this principle I learned – the understanding of science, and its application to patients in a rewarding and meaningful way, was theoretically a perfect combination. However, at that time I was not too sure about how I would cope with things like seeing blood, or small things such as how much the pay was, and what the working life was like. I therefore arranged a work experience in a general medicine ward in Charing Cross hospital, where I had all of these questions answered and more. I was inspired by the scientific approach of the doctors when talking among themselves, but also by the down-to-earth and genuine kindness that they showed to each and every patient. The only other person who I had seen enjoy his job quite as much was my old biology teacher who was my inspiration in the first place. Taking aside the influences of these inspirational figures, I think medicine is a perfect fit for my interests; a pursuit of science, an application to the real world in a meaningful way, and day-to-day interaction with people. That is why I am trying my hardest to win a place in medical school and pursue this combination of interests which I am passionate about.'

Points to note

This student references influential figures, but also is quick to point out that his desire to study medicine is not only derived from them, but from his interests in the various facets of medical practice.

2. Can you tell us about yourself?

These two points would help you approach this question: use the rule of threes – select your strongest three characteristics and construct an answer based around them; and make sure you support your claims with solid and interesting examples.

> ### THE RULE OF THREES
>
> Students are often concerned about how many points to make in open questions such as 'Can you tell us about yourself?' Clearly there are an innumerate number of ways to describe oneself, from the physical, mental, spiritual, past, present and future. A rule that will help to save you from acute anxiety attacks due to open questions is the rule of threes. This states that if you are in doubt, you are best off giving three examples of whatever the question states. The reasoning behind it is that you want to strike a balance between appearing as if you know too little and boring the panel to tears. One example is usually too narrowly focused, two represents 'just a couple' of ideas and three is the optimal number. If you give more than three examples you may risk spreading yourself too thinly, speaking about too many topics at once or simply talking for too long on one subject. The panel wishes to see that you can summarize the important and relevant points in answering a question. Of course, one can think of many exceptions to this rule, but if the panic takes hold of you during the interview, this is a good principle to fall back on.

Example answer

'My name is Jane, I'm an A-level student studying chemistry, biology, physics and maths. I would say the three most important things about me are that I am determined, scientific and compassionate. I would say my determination to pursue a career in medicine is best understood if you know my family background. When I first considered studying medicine due to my interest in science, my parents actively discouraged me from taking the course as they believed it would be difficult to maintain a family life. I have actually looked into other careers such as accountancy, and done a work experience placement shadowing a tax accountant. However, it was easy for me to make the choice to pursue medicine after my work experiences on a urological surgery team, and with a respiratory medicine team in the Manchester Royal Infirmary, where I saw the excitement of stimulating work, the joy of helping patients and the challenge of interpreting studies, blood and urine tests combine with the patient's story to determine what was the diagnosis. Since then I have spent many nights arguing with my parents to allow me to study medicine, and finally they have supported me after seeing how enthusiastic I was in arranging more work experiences, and going on the Medsim medical course in Nottingham.

In terms of science, not only do I enjoy actively participating in class in all my science A levels, but I also enjoy reading the New Scientist *and the* Student BMJ. *I have a fellow applicant in my form class and we have a habit of telling each other the "story of the week" on Monday mornings after reading something interesting about science at the weekend. I find it helpful to try to explain a complex article I have read and also be challenged by questions about it. My form tutor is a biology teacher, so when we get stuck we often trouble him with further questions.*

In terms of compassion, I have had some good experience in a school programme that involves reading for the blind, and I forged a close friendship with my allocated reading-recipient, and talked about her life and how difficult things were during times of rationing, and when she lost her husband. However, I think my compassion is best reflected in the day-to-day way I live my life, and small things such as helping to explain science concepts to classmates who are finding things more difficult are things that I enjoy doing and I hope to bring that attitude to my study of medicine at university.'

Points to note

This student uses well-backed-up points to illustrate the 'big three' elements (dedicated, scientific and compassionate) that she described about her personality. Can you recap in one sentence what the three elements were?

She manages to maintain interest from the interview panel with a unique and interesting anecdote about her scientific discussion with her friend and then goes on to reflect about her feelings on it. This is a good example of DPT in action.

3. Can you take us through your personal statement?

In order to prepare for this question, you must know your personal statement word for word. It is also helpful if you have geared your personal statement towards the specific medical school to which you are applying. (See *How to Get into Medical School*, published by Kogan Page, for further information on the design of a differentiated personal statement.) This will allow you to tie in the evidence you have submitted on paper with your statements and with the particular course on which you are about to embark.

You can use this question to demonstrate your communication skills, by organizing your answer into a well-structured format.

Example answer

'I would like to highlight two contrasting areas, which are the academic and extra-curricular activities sections. In terms of academia, I would say that one of the more unique features is my A level in Latin. I studied it mostly out of intellectual curiosity and enjoyment but recently I have come to realize it may be practical for the study of medicine too. For example "thalamus" means "inner bedroom", but also refers to the part of the brain between the midbrain and the forebrain, and looks anatomically like the inner bedroom of the brain itself. I believe that having an understanding of the etymology of words could be helpful in my study of medicine. I do enjoy

biology and chemistry and have been involved with several extra-curricular projects, the last of which was a presentation on the biology of common overdoses, such as of paracetamol and alcohol, and their effects on the body. I found these presentations interesting to research and in trying to answer the questions from my classmates after the talk.

My main extra-curricular interest is acting, and I have performed a variety of roles from backing singer to co-star of the school play. I have also been involved in the school's improvised comedy show, which involved a demanding use of observational humour. I enjoyed having to think on my feet, and responding to the feelings of the crowd as to when to keep going, and when to change tack.

In both arenas, the element of communication has been vital and I have enjoyed learning to express myself in both a comedic and scientific sense.'

Points to note

- Try and draw the panel's attention to particularly unique features and your 'best' achievements.

- You can use the principles of DPT to construct an interesting anecdote about a particular achievement of yours. This is a good way to maintain interest from the interviewers and to make your interaction with them stand out from their interactions with all of the previous candidates.

- The candidate uses c-chain manipulation with cadence to steer the conversation towards communication skills.

4. Why do you want to be a doctor?

This question has some key similarities to question 1 and you can use the main themes noted for that question to construct your answer to this one. However, it is important to note some key differences.

It is specifically asking you about being a doctor, and so it is important to reference you aims and ambitions towards the career rather than the training. In contrast, in answering 'Why do you want to study medicine?' you could spend more time discussing your intellectual interest in the subject matter, such as biology and physiology.

You can use this opportunity to introduce your deeper understanding of medicine, including the advantages and disadvantages of the career. This may lead on to follow-up questions about life as a doctor, which you should be prepared for.

5. What do you want to achieve in medicine?

Example answer

'I would say my aims in medicine may change as my career in medicine progresses. I am not sure exactly what branch of medicine I wish to go into but at the moment I am interested in surgery. Therefore, when I am starting out, I mainly want to safely care for and treat my patients with either surgery or medications. My main reward will be the health and happiness of each individual patient. As I become more senior, I might be able to make an impact on a larger population of people by doing some research that may show, for example, which treatments are more effective than others, therefore helping more than just the people I see face to face.

I remember one particular conversation with one of the consultants on my general surgery work experience who said that he very much enjoyed the teaching element of his job, and I thought that this was something that in the future I might look forward to being involved in. By teaching both medical students and junior doctors I could potentially be helping all the patients who come under their care both then and in the future. Finally, I think every aspiring doctor wants to invent a drug or procedure that will cure a major disease such as cancer – I think it is probably unlikely that it would be me, but I think at this stage there isn't any harm in me aiming high and trying my best to help the most people that I can to the best of my ability.'

Points to note

Note how this candidate has structured his answer along both a chronological and numerical pattern. He is also making use of chain theory to execute c-chain manipulation towards his work experience. In particular, he uses cadence to emphasize one conversation during his work experience and reflect on his personal feeling about it, which may make the interviewers more likely to pick up on this cue.

Additional things you may wish to achieve in medicine that you can discuss include:

- international work, helping those in less economically developed countries;
- aid work, helping international relief efforts and disaster management;
- research – looking in depth into new potential medications or enriching our understanding of the human body via research.

Less common answers

These might include using information technology – using advances in computing to change the way we store and interpret data or investigating the use of robotics in surgery; or becoming a cruise ship doctor – enjoying a lifestyle of touring the world on cruise ships while treating people who need help on board.

6. If you were to become a doctor, how would you wish your patients to describe you, and why?

Example answer

'Of all the descriptions, I would probably say professional, caring and humorous. Professional, because I believe that on the job our first duty is always to the patient and this commitment should be both taken seriously and performed diligently. Caring, because within this setting of delivering health care, it is best performed if we have a good doctor–patient relationship, as well as giving a sense of personal achievement on the job. Humorous, because laugher is the best medicine, when used in conjunction with evidence-based medical therapy.'

Points to note

Note the introductory element to the answer that lists the characteristics the student will go on to discuss; this makes it easier for the interviewers to follow where he is in the answer and when the end point may occur, so it does not appear to be an endless stream of talking. This is aided by the student's use of the rule of threes here. He is also using cadence to steer the later conversation towards a discussion about evidence-based medicine.

Consider the following attributes:

- professional;
- capable;
- polite;
- caring;
- good communicator;
- strong leader;
- good team worker;
- humorous.

Note that being 'humorous' is very different from simply being 'funny'; if you choose to use humour in your answers, make sure it is sophisticated and not flippant.

Realistic ambition

7. How have you prepared to study medicine?

This question requires you to refer to activities you have undertaken that are specifically related to preparing to study medicine. This may include:

- speaking to current doctors, to discuss working life and the advantages and disadvantages of being a doctor;

- speaking to current medical students;

- work experience placement;

- voluntary work;

- outside reading – reading medical journals and medical news, for example the *British Medical Journal* (*BMJ*); scientific news, for example *New Scientist*; and medically-related books, for example *The Selfish Gene* by Richard Dawkins;

- extra-curricular activities with a medical or scientific focus such as through a school medical or scientific society.

8. Why do you want to be a doctor, rather than enter another profession that is caring or intellectually challenging?

Examples of other caring professionals include:

- nurses;

- health care assistants;

- social workers;

- counsellors.

People working in intellectually challenging professions include:

- physicists or chemists;

- engineers;

- research scientists.

These features are special to the job of a doctor:

- Trust – people tend to trust their doctors and this kind of relationship can be rare even in other caring professions.

- The combination of an intellectually challenging job with daily interaction with people and a caring profession is also rare in other jobs.

- Teaching and research are increasingly forming an important element of the job. These are less frequently associated with the other caring professions as listed above.

- The variety within medicine itself means that you can choose a specialty involving hospital lifestyle, a community-based (GP) lifestyle or spending time in operating theatres or laboratories, according to your personal preferences.

There are also some features that are quantitatively different from those of the other professions; that is, they are present in other careers, but greater in amount for doctors:

- Working lifestyle – the European Working Directive limits the hours of doctors and sets specific conditions regarding rest breaks, annual leave and rest between shifts. This has improved the work–life balance of the profession, although the actual working lifestyle can vary highly between specialties. For example, accident and emergency departments often operate shift-based systems. Rheumatologists, on the other hand, might perform most of their ward and clinic work between 9 am and 5 pm, and might be needed less often out of these hours.

- Economics – being a doctor is reasonably well-rewarded financially and higher paying than most of the other caring professions. There is scope for private work to increase this benefit.

- Biology – there are several other intellectually challenging fields related to biology, such as veterinary medicine, and marine biology, but none with more of a focus on the human body than medicine itself.

9. Why do you believe you have the ability to undertake the study and work involved in becoming a doctor?

The question specifies that the ability is related to the study and work involved and requires that you demonstrate this using examples to underline your point. Examples you could use might be of intellectual ability:

- grades;

- other examinations;

- science or maths challenges, Olympiads.

Alternatively, you might talk about activities that demonstrate commitment. Examples might be achievement or perseverance with an extra-curricular activity, or long-standing endeavour in a worthwhile activity, for example community work or voluntary work.

> Questions of the same type as question 9 are amenable to the use of DPT, not only to show evidence for your answer, but also to maintain interest.

10. What do you think being a doctor entails, apart from treating patients?

This question is looking for whether or not you have a broad understanding of what life as a doctor will be like, not only the day-to-day practicalities of the job.
Consider the following areas:

- civic responsibility;

- assisting in emergency situations;

- acting as a character referee or witness;

- taking care of your own health;

- promoting healthy lifestyles;

- teaching junior doctors;

- keeping up to date with best medical practice.

Example answer

'A doctor is part of the health care system, and this means that you will work as part of a team, and have to be responsible towards the others in terms of support, teaching and even simple socializing. A doctor's role also includes civic responsibility. There is a degree of responsibility in how one conducts oneself in daily life. Any criminal offences, in particular involving illegal drugs or heavy alcohol use, may cause a decreased performance on the job, and can lead to disciplinary measures or dismissal.

In situations outside of the workplace, most infamously on aeroplanes, but also in road traffic accidents or simply in restaurants or shops, you may be called upon to attend to the health of a member of the public in an emergency situation. Appearance is another consideration, as unusual or extrovert clothing, jewellery, make-up or hairstyle may be less accepted than in other jobs. Responsibility for your own health is important as it can have an impact on the health care you deliver to patients; you must be registered with a GP, and beware when coming into work with potentially infectious conditions. Finally, it is also to important to make time for family, hobbies, interests, travel and enjoying life, as a vital part of a sustainable career as a doctor.'

11. What branch of medicine do you think would interest you? Why?

Be prepared to discuss the branches of medicine you know well. You should have a broad understanding of the different departments and what the job entails. There are several main divisions in the practice of medicine that you could comment on, the first of which being hospital medicine versus community medicine. Essentially community medicine is based around the GP, who sees the patients either for treatment or for referral to a specialist. Hospital medicine is made up of specialist consultants who treat patients with conditions relevant to the consultants' body of knowledge and expertise. The next main divide is between medicine and surgery. This broadly encompasses treatment via medications or treatment via operation.

You could therefore comment on whether you would enjoy more the prospect of community or hospital medicine, or life as a GP. If you have done a work experience placement in a particular specialty, you can link this into your answer, which might give you some additional reasons for your interest. These can include inspirational doctors, interesting cases, knowledge of the lifestyle of the doctors in that specialty or academic intrigue.

Avoid committing yourself too firmly to one path. Medical students and even junior doctors do not always know which branch of medicine they want to pursue, and their ideas are likely to change during the course of medical school.

12. What steps have you taken to try to find out whether you really do want to become a doctor?

This question is similar in nature to question 7 and you can use a similar approach to tackle this one. However, there are some additional points for consideration, as this question is testing whether or not you have made a realistic assessment of your desire to become a doctor.

You may find it helpful to refer to the following:

- Laboratory experience. This is important because you may be more interested in the scientific and academic elements of medicine, and a work experience in a laboratory may influence you to pursue a career in academia by undertaking a pure science degree, and going to undertake a PhD. You may find that you prefer the combination of the intellectual pursuit with patient contact, but having this experience would allow you to compare and contrast with your medical work experience to give a balanced answer.

- Other types of work experience. In a similar way, work experience in a bank, law firm or other profession may help to draw this contrast between other professions and medicine that you could discuss and that might have firmed up your decision to become a doctor. You may find it helpful to undertake such work experiences earlier on, and focus more on medical work experience later as it will reinforce the fact that you have taken your time to decide on medicine, but once you did, you were very focused on that goal.

- Discussion with current doctors. It is important to know exactly what you are signing up for, and one of the best ways to do this is by learning from the people who are currently on the job. You can use DPT to construct an anecdote about one of your discussions that you found most helpful and use cadence to guide it towards a topic of your choosing.

13. How do you think medicine differs from other health professions?

This question is similar to question 8, and you can use the frameworks there to form the foundations for your answer. However, you should not only focus on reporting the factual differences, but also try to add a personal perspective to the answer.
Other health professionals include:

- nurses;
- health care assistants;
- physiotherapists;
- dieticians;
- pharmacists;
- occupational therapists.

Try to integrate your own experiences into your answer about other health professions. For example, you may have seen the day-to-day jobs of nurses or health care assistants on the wards. Reflect on these experiences in your answer.

14. How old are you when you become a consultant?

Use this chance to demonstrate rational explanation.

Example answer

'Based on a five-year university course, two years as a foundation doctor and six years as a specialist trainee, the total length of training is around 13 years. Factoring in possibilities such as an intercalated BSc at undergraduate level, or a year in research as a specialist trainee, and taking the average age of entry of a student to be 18, I would estimate the range to be from 31 to 33 years old.'

This demonstrates your knowledge of the medical training system well, and awareness of research in the career of a doctor. It gives a good structured framework, showing the reasoning of your answer. Giving a range as the answer displays some awareness of statistics and scientific methodology, handling uncertainty in a scientific manner rather than just giving a point estimate.

15. How long does medical training take?

See the answer to question 14 for the average framework. Bear these points in mind:

- Graduate courses take four years.

- It is possible to integrate a PhD into a medical degree at some universities, which results in a nine-year course.

- The foundation programme after graduation takes two years, where a junior doctor undertakes a variety of placements in different specialties to gain a broad experience.

- Specialist training takes six years, but may take longer if some time is spent in research or training for a higher degree, such as an MA in education.

16. What can you tell me about the average week of a surgeon?

> **Interviewer**: 'What can you tell me about the average week of a surgeon?'
>
> **Candidate**: 'Well it depends on what type of surgeon.' (Pause.) 'There's a lot of variation between different types, and they can be quite different.' (Long pause.) 'Brain surgeons do a lot of very delicate work.'
>
> **Interviewer (impatiently)**: 'Would you care to describe the work of at least one type?'
>
> This student would undoubtedly irritate the interview panel by his lack of attempting to say anything concrete, and this is a common mistake, especially among less-well-prepared candidates. In this case, the student asked me what he had done wrong, as he felt he had been trying to answer the question, but not been given the chance. I told him that although it was true that his answer was correct, it had not imparted very much information to the interviewer. We worked through some of the following points and the vastly improved answer that he gave in a subsequent interview is listed on the next page. Avoid making the same mistake by ensuring that you give solid examples.

This kind of question gives many different kinds of opportunity. First, it gives you the opportunity to show that you can organize information and present it in some kind of order. This skill is very important for junior doctors who are presenting information about a patient to a more senior doctor for consideration; a jumbled answer will give responses varying from a disapproving look to a severe interrogation. Second, it gives you the opportunity to speak about your work experience, and to demonstrate not only that you have done some placements but also that you have actually learned from them.

Organization
The key principles are to take your time and consider the question and the various aspects of the answer. Avoid the temptation simply to blurt out the first thing that comes to mind. Second, think of a way to organize your answer. Third, make sure what you are saying is broad enough so it is hard to be picked up as wrong. If you have a relevant experience, introduce it here, and be ready to talk about it further as a follow-up question.

Example answer

'The average week of a surgeon will involve some combination of operations in theatre, as well as preoperative work and post-operative care on the wards. There would also be some clinics where the surgeon sees patients from outside the hospital for consideration of surgical treatment. On my work experience, I saw that junior doctors would be more involved in ward work, middle-grade doctors in clinics and training for operations, and consultants in clinics and operations. Surgeons may also be involved in multidisciplinary meetings with medical doctors, for example for cancer patients, because their treatment can be complex.'

These are the key features of this answer:

- It is easy to defend – saying 'some combination of' is better than giving specific proportions.

- It is stratified; in this case the candidate has chosen seniority level to break down his answer to refer to junior, middle-grade and senior surgeons.

- The comments are 'outside of the box'. Surgeons are not an entity entirely unto themselves; they do have important interactions with the medical doctors. Their opinion may also be requested about a patient on a medical ward if it is considered that the patient may have a surgical problem.

17. Can you describe the average week of a doctor?

Use the hints and tips from the above questions to see if you can use these principles to describe the average week of a medical doctor.

Other than seeing patients, activities undertaken may include:

- research;
- auditing;
- departmental meetings;
- teaching medical students and junior doctors;
- speaking to patients' relatives;
- unusual or nasty questions.

18. What would you most like us to ask you in this interview?

This is an unusual question, but actually represents a golden opportunity to select the question you feel most comfortable answering. There are almost 200 other questions in this book, so choose wisely!

Try to have a feeling for your strengths and weaknesses from discussion with other candidates. You can estimate this by speaking to your peers about their applications and what they feel about their good and bad points. You can then choose your question.

19. What things do you think might make people inclined to drop out of medical training?

Factors that you may wish to consider include:

- stress;
- working hours;
- having made the wrong career choice;
- physical health issues;
- family issues;
- financial issues.

20. Why should we pick you rather than other, better qualified candidates?

We looked at this question in the a-chain navigation section in Chapter 2 – the key framework of a thinking pause, acknowledging the situation, presenting arguments for and against and then coming to a balanced conclusion can be used here.

Example answer

'I would say that the qualifications required for medicine include academic ones, as well as those regarding teamwork, leadership, communication skills, empathy and dedication. Therefore, I do appreciate that there will be candidates who are better qualified in all of these fields than me, and others who are better qualified in some but not all of them. On the other hand, I also believe that I have worked hard to become a rounded academic and compassionate candidate, and therefore I hope I am better qualified than some others as well. Taking into

consideration the candidates who are better qualified than me on paper, I think there are some intangible qualities that I will bring to the course that are harder to measure, and the most significant of these is my interest and desire to study medicine. This is not a formal qualification, but something that I can only express in my words and actions up until now. Therefore, I sincerely hope you will pick me, and I hope to demonstrate that this desire to study medicine will help make me an excellent medical student and future doctor, even in the face of my strong competition.'

21. How might you put someone off a career in medicine?

Example answer

'In some ways it would be difficult for me to put someone off medicine as I am so enthusiastic about it! However, I think that different people desire different things from their career, and I would highlight some of the difficulties and negatives about medicine in order to put them off. I might start with the physical elements, which involve seeing blood, injuries and suffering, and potentially working in areas where you are exposed to bodily fluids with their associated unpleasantness. Life as a doctor may be unlike that of a normal office nine-to-five job, and you may be required to work on-call shifts that would include evenings, weekends and nights. This might make other commitments, such as those to family, more difficult. There are some physical dangers such as exposure to disease, some economic hazards such as being sued by patients and some emotional hazards such as witnessing death, or causing harm as a result of medical error. However, it would still be difficult for me to put someone off, mostly because I am genuinely looking forward to it, and it would be difficult for this enthusiasm not to come across.'

The negative sides of medicine include:

- being on call and doing evening, weekend and night work;
- physical dangers such as needlestick injuries and infectious diseases;
- geographical instability – since there is national competition for doctors;
- the necessity for lifelong learning and many years of examinations;
- emotional aspects – seeing suffering and death;
- the risk of being sued or struck off for poor practice.

(For more details see question 71.)

Summary

- This chapter contains some of the most frequently asked questions at medical school interview, so become very familiar with them and prepare carefully.

- Undertake the learning tasks to improve your performance in delivery of answers.

- You must know your personal statement inside out, and the intelligent student will anticipate which areas may be further explored.

- These questions tend to occur at the beginning of the interview, and therefore form your first impression. It is vital that you slow down, take your time, and give interesting and informative answers to maximize this impression.

CHAPTER 4

The Multiple Mini-Interview

The Multiple Mini-Interview (MMI) is a novel method of assessment being adopted with increasing frequency by medical schools. A departure from the traditional method, it requires its own form of unique preparation. This chapter will describe what it is and why it is used. It will cover how to prepare, and critically demonstrate how objective marking sheets are used, which will influence how you approach the station. A sample transcript gives insight into how an MMI station looks in real life. Example questions are worked through in detail and by type. Finally, some important practice techniques are discussed.

What is it?

The MMI is markedly different from the traditional medical school interview which features a long session in front of a fixed panel of interviewers. The best way to imagine the MMI is like a game show, with multiple rounds of challenges which need to be passed. Of course, the prize is a coveted place at medical school. Each challenge is called a 'station', and is a self-contained mini-interview with at least one interviewer or examiner, along with medical students or actors.

Each station is different, and lasts between 5 and 10 minutes, typically around 7. It sets a scenario, placing you in a challenging position such as a doctor choosing between patients you might save, or breaking bad news to a family. It might be consoling an upset peer, or allocating a hospital budget. Almost any type of scenario is possible, although the stations are designed to test specific criteria as described below.

Often current medical students are used as part of the station, and may pretend to be a patient, a relative, a senior doctor, nurse, lawyer, pharmacist, policeman, student, criminal or whatever the station demands.

Most MMI circuits are between 7 and 12 stations long, meaning your 'testing' period can last up to one and a half hours or more. This is significantly more challenging than a traditional interview, which usually lasts 20 to 30 minutes, and involves you sitting and talking to the same faces. The complexity of the MMI means you are constantly on your feet and moving to the next station, one minute pretending to be a junior doctor, the next a medical student. You will need to learn how to quickly switch roles, digest a scenario and improvise, and then do it over again. This chapter is designed to help maximize your ability to meet this challenge.

Why is it used?

i) *It is more objective than normal interviews*
    Having different examiners assess you independently at each station gives a more balanced view than a few interviewers in a panel. Many MMIs use an objective scoring sheet (described below).

ii) *It tests applied rather than reported skills*
    Questions such as 'give examples of when you showed empathy' or 'are you a good communicator' become less relevant as interviewers can see your empathy or communication skills first-hand.

iii) *It is compartmentalized*
    If an interviewee gives a single terrible answer, or gets off to a bad start, this can colour the whole interview for both themselves and the interview panel.
    However, in an MMI, the problem is 'contained' to one station, and the next examiner will never know how bad (or fantastic!) you were at the last station.

As of 2014, the following universities use an MMI format interview: Aberdeen, Cardiff, St George's, Dundee, Birmingham, East Anglia, Keele, Manchester and Queen's Belfast. Since the evidence that MMIs offer a superior selection process in many ways to a traditional interview, this list is expected to expand in the near future. Ensure that you check your intended institution's policy thoroughly.

How to prepare

Your MMI preparation can be divided into two main arms: general preparation and technical preparation.

General preparation has significant overlap with your traditional medical school interview preparation because there are many fundamental similarities. The subject matter which might come up, from current NHS issues, ethical conundrums, future educational issues, teamwork, leadership and so on, will still be potentially examined in this format. Therefore, the basic principles described in previous chapters will be useful in this setting. Additionally, looking through the question and answers will offer good insight into the type of problems which will come up.

However, there are some technical aspects of preparation which will be important to your success beyond your general preparation. These are best understood by looking at how scores are allocated in MMI. One of the goals of using MMIs is to be objective, and therefore examiners almost always use a pre-determined score sheet which lists areas for which students can gain marks. Such a mark sheet might appear as follows:

Station 1

2 minute reading time

Task

You are the F2 doctor in an accident and emergency department. You are treating two members of a family who have all been in a serious car accident. Mr Smith is a 52-year-old male who is the most severely injured, sustaining fractures to both of his legs, and losing a lot of blood. He is currently being transferred to the operating theatre to have his the fractures fixed and stem the blood loss. His wife Mrs Smith was less severely injured, but has multiple cuts and lacerations, as well as extensive bruising over her body. She is recovering in the department. Their 16-year-old daughter, Jenny, has just been brought to your department by her teacher, and you are instructed by the consultant to inform her about the situation. (five minutes)

Marking scheme for station 1

	Task	Good	Adequate	Not done/ inadequate
		Yes (2)	Yes, but (1)	No (0)
	Introduction			
1.	Greets daughter, checks identity			
2.	Introduces self and role			
3.	Explains reasons for coming to talk to daughter			
	Explanation			
4.	Establishes starting point of daughter – what does she know so far?			
5.	Introduces the information sensitively (warning shot)			
6.	Gives relevant information of appropriate length			
	Empathy			
7.	Recognizes important non-verbal cues from daughter			
8.	Gives time and space for patient to react			
9.	Acknowledges the feelings and emotions			
10.	Asks what further information she would like to know			
	Organization and behaviour			
11.	Organizes information in a logical sequence			
12.	Uses appropriate non-verbal supporting behaviour			
13.	Appropriate tone, pace and language			

Additional examiner comments

_____

_____

Total Score _____

As you can see from the above marking scheme, having a technical approach to each station can help you score *widely* and well as in depth. Looking at the points under the category of 'Introduction', for example, reveals some interesting learning points. It may not be obvious to introduce yourself, your name and your role, as well as checking that the person you are speaking to is the correct person. Even if it is obvious, if you are not in the habit of doing it, it is very easy to miss out this step if your mind is focused on simply telling the daughter the facts of the case.

Therefore, one key element of MMI practice is getting used to a routine. When you meet a new person as a doctor or medical student, you should always quickly and clearly introduce who you are, what you role is, and why you are speaking to the patient or relative. As you get into this habit, you will be able to be natural with your tone and gestures. It will also become second nature, allowing you more time to focus on thinking about the scenario itself.

Sample transcript

Student (S)

Daughter (D)

S: Hi, my name is Chris, I'm a doctor in the accident and emergency department, and I've come to speak to you about your parents. Can I just check that you are Jenny Smith?

D: Yes, I'm Jenny.

S: Ok Jenny, can I take a seat?

D: Sure, go ahead.

S: I know you've just arrived at our hospital Jenny, do you know why you have been brought here today?

D: Actually I was in school and the police called my teacher, she told me my parents were in an accident, and they took me straight here. What's going on? [looks upset]

S: Ok Jenny, I'm afraid I have a bit of bad news. As you have mentioned, your parents have been injured in a car accident. We are currently treating them in the department now. Your mum has some minor injuries, some cuts and bruising but she is otherwise fine. Your dad was a bit more seriously injured, and he is just going up to the operating theatre where our surgeons are going to treat him.

D: Oh my god. [sobs] Is my dad going to survive? What operation is he having?

S: Your dad injured his legs in the accident, and broke his bones. What we need to do is fix the bones because when they are broken sometimes they can bleed quite a lot. We are doing that right now, and giving him blood transfusions as well. I'm sure he will be ok, we've got some great surgeons here and they are doing everything they can.

D: [Continues crying for a while] So you are saying he's going to live? But will he be able to walk again? He needs to drive for work you know...

S: He is being treated right now, and I am confident he will make it through. We will know much more once the surgeons have helped to fix him up.

D: So you are saying there's a chance he won't be able to walk?

S: Erm, he has had a serious injury, so I do not want to give you the wrong information right now. What I can say is that we do treat a lot of bone fractures here, and although the recovery can take a while, really most of our patients are able to walk again. The orthopaedic surgeon in charge will be able to tell you more once the operation is complete.

D: I'm so worried. Why did this have to happen to them!

S: I'm so sorry this has happened to your parents. I understand you must be feeling very upset right now. [Pause] Is there anything I can do for you?

D: [Pause] When can I see my mum?

S: I will go through and check how she's doing, if she's stable I hope we can bring you through as soon as possible.

D: Thanks a lot.

S: Is there anything else you would like me to do or explain for you?

D: No that's OK, I just want to see my mum now.

END

Transcript analysis

The student in this transcript gets off to a good start. He introduces himself and his role, and checks the identity of the daughter. Rather than diving straight in, he establishes what she knows first, and then introduces the idea that bad news is forthcoming. He structures the data well, firstly telling her that her mother is generally OK after having some minor injuries. He then tackles the issue of the father, using simple language and not going into too much detail at once. Notice how he says 'he is just going up to the operating theatre where our surgeons are going to treat him', where many students would be tempted to jump in with details of fractures and blood loss. This gives some time and space for the 16-year-old to process the information, in chunks rather than all at once. He later explains things clearly, and jargon free ('broke his bones' rather than 'sustained multiple fractures').

However, later in the station, the student gets a bit flustered by the question 'So you are saying there's a chance he won't be able to walk?' He deals with it quite well, explaining how he does not want to give out incorrect information. However, you can see that he slips into jargon here, using 'fractures' and quite unnecessarily 'orthopaedic surgeon'. If you refer to the mark sheet, you can see why he would score a '1' under item 13 (appropriate tone, pace and language). He has generally used them well, and under the score of adequate the description reads 'yes, but'.

Eventually he recovers, leaving pauses for the daughter to express her grief, and offering further explanation (scored under item 10).

This example should highlight why a technical approach is needed for MMIs. Most medical students should manage a reasonably empathetic tone of voice, and be good at explaining medical information. However, it is easy to forget to pause and allow space, to keep jargon-free, to check her understanding and to verbally acknowledge her feelings ('*I understand you must be feeling very upset right now. [Pause]*').

The following example MMI questions will guide you through some of the key points to remember.

Example questions by category

i) Decision making under difficult circumstances

ii) Empathy

iii) Ethical problems

iv) Capacity to cope with the curriculum and course

v) Communication skills stations

vi) Challenging situations

vii) Non-interactive stations

i) *Decision making under difficult circumstances*

Prioritization problems

Managing one's time is a critical skill for a clinician. In hospital, you will often have to face multiple demands on your time, and being able to organize them in an efficient manner is vital. Significant mismanagement can cause accidents or serious harm if deadlines for treatments of individual patients are missed if you are too busy with another less urgent task. Therefore, such questions are frequent occurrences in MMIs. Consider the follow example:

Station 2

You are a junior doctor on a cardiology ward. You are attending to a patient who needs blood samples taken and sent to the laboratory by 3pm, which is in 20 minutes time, in order to be ready for the next day for the consultant ward round. He has small and tricky veins, and you are having trouble obtaining the blood samples you need. A nurse comes in to tell you that the relatives of a patient who died from an acute myocardial infarction yesterday have come to see you about collecting his death certificate. Unfortunately, no one told you they arrived an hour ago, and they are getting very upset and frustrated that they have been kept waiting. They are now threatening to make a complaint about you to the hospital. What do you do?

Common Pitfalls

Some students might take the line of finishing their blood sample taking, which is important for the 'living' patient, and dealing with the 'dead' patient afterwards. Whilst this might be practical, remember that you are being scored on your ability to communicate your decision making. You should make each step of your thinking clear, justified and rational. You may wish to consider:

a) Recognizing that there is a dilemma, and that the suffering of patients' relatives, particularly grieving ones, is not a trivial matter.

b) Balance this fact with the fact that another patient has an urgent clinical matter which needs attention.

c) It is a complex task, and since you are already there, with equipment prepared, and searching for small veins, it is reasonable to try and finish the procedure.

d) However, kindly ask the nurse to explain your situation, and apologize.

e) Once you have finished the procedure, also apologize and attend to the relatives.

f) In MMIs, the actor may threaten you with a complaint in person. In this case, it is best to explain that they are totally within their rights to complain, but you would like to help them now that you are there. Acknowledging their loss and grief may go some way to helping the scenario.

ii) *Empathy*

The empathy station can be considered an advanced version of the interview questions on this topic. Essentially, you will be given the opportunity to demonstrate how you interact as an empathetic person. Consider the following station:

Station 3

You are a first year medical student, and after one of your lectures, you notice that there is a fellow student who is waiting behind, and crying by himself. How would you act in this situation?

Common pitfalls

This type of station does not reveal much in the initial information. This should prompt you that you will be doing more information gathering than information giving in this station. All you know is that someone is upset; before you can start being of help, you need to develop some rapport and give space for that person to express their reasons. You can bet that there will be more marks for empathetic listening, pauses, appropriate gestures and tone than there will be for coming up with concrete solutions for their problems.

You may wish to consider:

a) An opening which builds rapport in a non-invasive way eg '*Hi I'm Chris, we're in the same class but I don't think we've met. I just came over to see if you are ok.*' Notice how this uses the principles of introducing self, role and reason as we have seen from the previous marking scheme, but does so in a gentle way.

b) Listen attentively; don't feel pressed to fill up any 'dead air' with the sound of your own talking. Be patient.

c) Use body language which you feel comfortable with. You may feel natural to put your hand on their shoulder or arm whilst comforting: this is fine, as long as you feel it is fine. Don't force such gestures as it is obvious if you are uncomfortable doing them.

iii) *Ethical problems*

The forms of ethical problems in MMI cases tend to be more urgent and immediate than in the normal interview setting. Discussions about general thoughts on euthanasia or abortion are replaced by scenarios where an ethical decision must be made within a limited time frame, often with a human consequence in front of you. Consider the following example:

Station 4

You are a medical student, running late for your final exam, when you spot someone collapsing in the street. During her fall, you notice that she bumped her head on the floor quite hard. It is early in the morning, and not many people are around. Unfortunately, you are on a last warning from the medical faculty for having missed classes and lectures during the year. You know that if you do not attend the examination, it is quite likely you will have to repeat the year, or have a more severe punishment applied including being ejected from the course altogether. What do you do?

Common pitfalls

This seems like an 'obvious' case, and many students will be tempted to pursue a line of reasoning such as 'I'd just miss the exam, and go and help the injured person' without a second thought. This is simplistic approach is not what the examiners are looking for! Remember the breadth of the marking sheets. Some points which may well be available include:

a) acknowledging the difficulty of the dilemma at hand;

b) weighing up the beneficence to the person with the future lives you might save if you were not kicked out of medical school;

c) considering methods of avoiding punishment, eg calling the medical school once the situation is safely dealt with.

You should quickly turn to the management of the injured person, and here is where some first aid principles may come in helpful:

d) firstly check for danger – why might the patient have fallen?

e) see if the patient is conscious;

f) see if they are bleeding;

g) check for any obvious injury;

h) call for help;

i) ask for helper to call an ambulance.

Remember not to stick to a rigid list. At any point, the examiner can throw a twist at you. He could say 'the patient smells heavily of alcohol, wakes up and tries to grab you', as equally as 'the patient seems to be bleeding profusely and has a weak and shallow pulse'. At all times, recognizing your limitations, and asking for help quickly, will stand you in good stead, in this scenario as well as life as doctor!

Simple statements such as 'I got into medical school to help people, so I would best demonstrate my suitability to be a doctor by helping the patient, and try to convince the dean not to kick me out later' may serve you best. Students who suggest more involved methods, such as getting phone numbers off witnesses to help testify to their involvement, or getting statements from the paramedics or even taking a smartphone video, are in a way missing the point. Save these creative but essentially self-serving points for the end of the station.

iv) *Capacity to cope with the curriculum and course*

Medical schools, and indeed life as a doctor in general, are based on collaborative learning. You will find that many MMI tasks relating to the curriculum are not based on learning alone, but on problems you may encounter with peers. Consider the following:

Station 5

You are a second year medical student in our University, and you have started the year in a new PBL group. One of your groupmates is constantly disruptive, messaging on her phone throughout the first session. You find that she does not prepare for the PBL sessions, and often gives brief and unhelpful answers when asked questions by the tutor. You notice that she simply takes the groups notes at the end of the session, and benefits without making much contribution. At the end of one of your sessions, you find yourself alone with her after everyone has left. What would you do?

Common Pitfalls

The text of the task is written in a plaintiff and accusing tone, giving you the impression you should in some way 'tell off' this person for their behaviour. However, since you are peers, it may not be ideal to take this approach. There are many reasons for messaging during class, and not putting in much effort. One of them is being a terrible student. However, others include personal issues, family problems, academic difficulties and many other things. Therefore, it is sensible to consider the following approaches:

a) Firstly, ask 'how are you doing?' or 'how are things with you lately?' The student may be prompted to reveal more about their situation.

b) Try to introduce the topic of work in a gentle fashion, eg 'I've noticed that you've been a bit distracted in our PBLs lately, is there anything going on?'

c) You can consider exploring avenues such as 'are you not enjoying this particular topic?' or 'how are you finding the tutor?'

d) If the actor reveals any information, remember to take time to acknowledge their feelings. It may be a case where the PBL topic is breast cancer, and the student's mother has just been diagnosed with it, for example.

The interviewers want to ensure that you can support your peers through a long and difficult course of study. Points for non-verbal communication, appropriate tone and language will mostly likely be in the mark scheme, so do not miss these out!

v) *Communication skills stations*

These stations allow you to prove what your personal statement most likely declares: that you are an excellent communicator. Consider the following scenario:

Station 6

You are the GP for a patient, Mr Brown, who is a 62-year-old male, has a BMI of 33, smokes, and drinks 30 units of alcohol per week. He comes to see you about a verruca on his foot, for which you prescribe appropriate treatment. It is now towards the end of your consultation, but you would like to spend six minutes talking to him about his lifestyle and how it relates to his health.

Common pitfalls

The scenario has given you a purposeful agenda: to discuss smoking, obesity and alcohol consumption. However, you must realize the limits of this. You are unlikely, in six minutes, to make a marked, lasting and permanent change to a 62-year-old man's life. What you can reasonably achieve, is getting him started on the process of thinking reflectively about his own life, and what changes he might need. Consider the following:

a) Your introduction to the topic should be sensitive and appropriate. 'Mr Brown, now that we have dealt with your foot, I wanted to have a quick chat about your general health. How do you feel about things at the moment?'

b) Broach one topic at a time: 'I'm just reading from the notes that you smoke, are you still smoking at the moment?'

c) Enquire, rather than challenge: 'Have you ever thought about quitting?' or 'are you ever worried about your drinking?'

d) Offer support: 'Could I offer any help in quitting?'

e) Listen, pick up on non-verbal cues and use non-verbal communication.

f) Try to avoid being prescriptive: rather than telling him he needs to do some running, ask him what forms of exercise he might enjoy.

vi) *Challenging situations*

Station 7

You are living in a student accommodation with a roommate. As winter approaches, you feel that the living room and bedroom of your flat are too cold to study, and you turn on the central heating when you get back from lectures. Your roommate tells you that central heating in small flats is a ridiculous waste of money and also bad for the environment. He promptly switches it off. After trying for a few days wearing a hat, coat and gloves indoors, you decide that you cannot study in such freezing conditions. You go and speak to your roommate about the situation.

Common pitfalls

You may or may not have experience of confrontation in your life. If you have, try to draw upon successful strategies. If you have not, avoid being drawn into heated arguments about saving the environment, and try to offer a compromise position which you can both accept. Consider the follow:

a) As usual, acknowledge the other person's position, as well as explaining your own.

b) Since you are both students, find the common ground and express your worries about it affecting your studies. You may find he is empathic to this at least.

c) Try to assess what the most serious concerns are. For example, if it is about money, it may be that he really cannot afford to pay for heating.

d) With this information, you can offer informed compromise positions, eg paying for the heating yourself, limiting the hours it is on etc.

e) Focus on the positives. Remember that (in the UK at least), it will not be a permanent problem, and the negotiation is only about a part of the year, not the whole year.

f) In very challenging situations, the actor may not compromise at all. He may flatly refuse any type of heating whatsoever. In such situations, show your examiner that you are resourceful and reasonable. Take this chance, with suggestions such as studying in the library, café or a friend's house, and purchasing a hot water bottle, which underline your adaptability.

vii) *Non-interactive stations*

There are occasionally stations which do not involve role-play, acting or situations. These stations are much more similar to standard interview questions, and may fall along the lines of:

Describe an example of when you demonstrated teamwork. What did you learn from it, and what will you improve on next time?

These stations will usually have only a single examiner, and in essence can be treated as normal interviews as discussed elsewhere in the book. Be aware that the time for your question is constrained to the limit of the MMI format, so budget your time accordingly. Also, there may be stations where you are presented with a graph, news article or ethical case to read and discuss. Again, refer to the question-and-answer section of the book for in-depth details of how to answer such questions. This underlines the importance of an all-round approach for interview preparation, even if you are primarily going for MMI universities.

Practice techniques

It is unusual to think of acting as having any role in medical interviews whatsoever. Most of the advice in this book relies on you giving genuine, well considered answers which are true to yourself. However, there is a specific circumstance in which your acting skills may be called upon, which is an interaction with a 'simulated patient'.

These are professional actors, or volunteer medical students, who are included as part of an MMI station to represent a person in a role play: typically a patient, but also relatives, a senior doctor, a nurse and so on. Their presence allows examiners to see first-hand how you interact with people in difficult situations.

It can be quite daunting to engage with a person who you know is pretending to have lost a loved one or have a terminal disease. This is perfectly understandable: you are not applying for a film academy, but a vocational degree. Nevertheless, such actors are also used in medical school as part of your communication skills training. It is important that you learn how to get into the reality of a role play, no matter how surreal it may feel.

The best way to do this is through practice. Performing role-plays with groups of friends is one of the best ways to achieve the necessary experience. You need at least three people: one for the examiner, one interviewee and one mock patient. Here are some practice scenarios to try out with your friends:

Practice Scenario 1:

You are a medical student studying for your end-of-year exam. Your hallmate tells you that he has been given the answer scheme to the exam by a friend, and offers you a copy. What would you do?

Practice Scenario 2:

You are an accident an emergency doctor, treating a 14-year-old girl. She has come to the department multiple times in the last year, and she seems to have several circular burns on her forearm which look like cigarette marks. She claims it was an accident in the kitchen, but you are worried that she might be the victim of abuse. Demonstrate how you would approach this problem.

Practice Scenario 3:

You are a high-school student on a work experience placement. You have been shadowing a junior doctor on a ward round who seems distracted and disorganized. When talking to you him, you notice the smell of alcohol on his breath. This has happened several times during your placement. You are now about to enter a room with the consultant of the team, for your end of placement review and feedback session. How might you bring up your concerns?

For each of the above scenarios, the 'actor' will need to participate fully and creatively to challenge you. They might play a confrontational student, who is scared of being reported for cheating. They may play a victim of abuse, or one who is more defensive and agitated. The source of abuse may be parents, a boyfriend or a gang. The consultant might be concerned or lenient. Learning to cope with unexpected, difficult scenarios will help your MMI performance, as will thinking about it from the 'examiners' side!

There is no doubt that when you first start practising, you might find it difficult to take it too seriously. Using 'make believe' to pretend to be sorry for a fake event, or pretending to be a character which is quite different from who you actually are, can feel silly. That is fine. Feel free to get your giggles and laughter out of the way in this early stage. It can be quite fun. It is far better to do this in the preparation stage than on the big day when it actually counts.

However, as you progress near the MMI date, you will need to develop the ability to stay in character. You must be able to sustain your image as the scenario demands, be it a junior doctor, medical student or otherwise, without letting the fact you are an interviewee in a fake situation become apparent. The following technique can help achieve this.

Interrupted sessions

During the course of one of your 5–10 minute scenarios, have the examiner deliberately stop you in a disruptive way. For example, calling the phone of the actor, and chatting to him, having both the actor and examiner leave the room or tell a joke to one another. This seems quite counter-intuitive way to train. However, what it critically practises is how to regain your composure and get back into the persona of a doctor after letting the role drop. Therefore, in your actual MMI, if you are disrupted by yourself or anything else, you will have some experience of taking a deep breath, and carrying on the role you are required to fulfil.

Use of online resources

The age of YouTube and Google Video is upon us, and they are an invaluable source of examples for MMI situations and how they work. Try to look at the scenario with a critical eye, and see what you might have done better than the example. Often, universities which use MMI also feature some examples on their website so that students can familiarize themselves with the format. Ensure that you take advantage of all of these additional resources.

Summary

- The MMI is a system of separate mini-challenges on different topics.

- It is uniquely challenging, needing the ability to swap between tasks rapidly.

- It requires skills in acting and role-play which traditional interviews do not.

- Knowledge of the objective marking scheme format allows you to anticipate areas where points might be scored.

- Group practice is a critical component of preparation.

CHAPTER 5

Work experience and voluntary work

Making the most of your work experience

One way in which students can consolidate their interest in medicine is to see the practice of medicine in action. It is usual for most applicants to have undertaken some work experience placements either in a hospital or in a GP setting. However, it is decidedly unusual for candidates to have put enough effort into the placement, and reflecting on their experience, to gain the most value from it for the application process, especially for interviews. Listed below are several ways in which you can maximize your work experiences.

Actively pursue information

Do not just turn up for the ride and expect to learn by osmosis. It is important that you actively pursue information – if you don't know what a disease is, or what an abbreviation stands for, you should ask. Ensure that you do this at an appropriate time, however. For example, if you are shadowing a ward round, your consultant might not appreciate being interrupted while examining or interacting with a patient. You may wish to save some questions to ask at the end of the ward round. However, the consultant may actively invite you to ask questions as you go along. It is a matter of preference, so be alert to the preferences of the team you are working with, as they can vary from person to person.

Learn about the good and bad sides of medical life

It will no doubt be interesting for you to learn the scientific and caring sides of the day-to-day work, but one of the other important pieces of information will be the difficulties faced by doctors. Make sure you talk to doctors of all grades and see the different types of experiences they have had.

See if there are current medical students around the wards, and talk to them about the good and bad sides of their course. This could also be helpful in selecting which medical school you wish to apply to, together with other considerations such as course type, length and location.

Spend time talking to patients

The ability to interact comfortably with your patients will be a very important skill throughout your career. Doctors of all levels will have to take a medical history from patients, which will be the first step in gathering information required to make a diagnosis. You will need to calm down distressed patients, explain results of investigations and medical conditions, break bad news and give advice on treatment. Although there is training in communication skills for such situations in most medical schools, you will be able to see if you enjoy talking to patients on the ward setting, even in an informal way. It may be helpful for you to discuss their medical conditions (with their consent) and in particular how their life has been affected by it.

Try to vary your activities

You may find it more stimulating and thought provoking to see a variety of new things, particularly if your attachment is long. Ask your team if it is possible to see some of the ward procedures such as chest drains, intravenous cannulations and catheter insertions. You may be allowed to sit in an outpatient clinic in which a doctor sees patients with conditions specific to their speciality. On a surgical placement, you may be able to go into the operating theatre. On a GP placement you could ask to accompany the GP on home visits to patients.

Keep a work experience diary

I recommend that you keep a work experience diary that you work on for just 10 minutes each day after you are finished at your placement. In it write down details of the following:

Medically-related stories of interest

These may be interesting medical conditions, rare diseases or common but important problems. You may wish to write down how the diagnosis is made, what the symptoms are and what tests are available to confirm the diagnosis.

Experiences of a medical career

You will have seen ward (or in the case of a GP, clinic) environments, and the day-to-day work that doctors do. Write down things that seem particularly interesting or relevant to interview questions in this book.

Patient-related stories

These entries will form an important part of the work experience diary when it comes to interview preparation. Admissions tutors will appreciate your effort of taking time to get to know patients and talking to patients about their experience of the medical world and also about their own condition and its impact on their life. Try to write down a relatively complete anecdote, for example as follows:

'I saw a patient on my work experience – JB – he was a 62-year-old man who was at the hospital with a fractured femur. He normally lives at home with his wife. I spoke to him about his time in hospital, and he said that one of the greatest fears he had was having general anaesthetic, and the thought of being asleep under the knife, rather than the pain of the incident itself. He was also afraid of not being able to walk again. I also spoke to one of the doctors who showed me how to compare both sides of the X-ray, to see that there was clearly a fracture. He also taught me that the blood supply to the top the femur can be interrupted by a fracture, and that this may cause the fracture fragment to die.'

WORK EXPERIENCE DIARY TEMPLATE

Attachment and date
Cardiology team, Lewisham Hospital

What did you learn from the day?
I was attached to the cardiology team, and followed them as they did the ward round and visited. I was shown a few ECGs, and it was explained to me that they are electrocardiograms, which are made by placing electrodes around the heart and measuring the electric current that is generated when the heart contracts. This can show if there are problems in conducting the electricity.

How did this affect you?

I quite enjoyed seeing how the biology of muscle contraction is applied in the everyday work of doctors in investigating patients. I began to see how my study of sciences will be important in my future career.

Any personal attributes witnessed in doctors or other members of staff?

Communication skills. The doctor I was following was the senior house officer, who was explaining his findings to a patient with chest pain. It was quite interesting to see how he reassured her that although she had a heart condition called angina (when you get heart pain from insufficient blood supply to the heart), this was quite different from having a heart attack as the damage was not permanent and heart tissue would not have died as a result.

He explained later that he wrote 'MI' – standing for myocardial infarction – in the notes, but advised me to avoid using medical jargon when talking to patients where possible as it can be distracting and confusing.

Additional notes

Write down important patient demographics

Include in your notes:

- age;
- sex;
- occupation;
- main medical diagnosis;
- other medical conditions;
- social history, for example whether the patient lives alone.

Remember to anonymize the data – never write down a patient's full name, just writing their initials will be sufficient.

NHS-related stories

It is now quite common for interviewers to ask for opinions about the NHS and it will therefore give a well-rounded impression if you can refer to something you have experienced, read about and thought about with regard to NHS issues. For example, a question that can come up is 'How has information technology had an impact on the NHS?'. Most students might theorize about the problems one might have with IT and some students may have read up on some problems. It is useful if you can do these things, but it might be easier and more accurate to discuss the experiences of the medical staff themselves. For example, you could mention the problems that doctors on the ward had with the IT systems in terms of slowness in electronic prescribing compared to the normal, hand-written medicine cards. (For more details see question 81.) This example demonstrates how keeping an efficient work experience diary can help to give you an advantage over candidates who may have done as much as you chronologically, but not maximized the benefits from it.

You may find that you have no events to write down for a particular day, which is fine. However, if this is happening frequently, it may be that you are not making the most of your attachment and you may wish to pursue talking to doctors and patients more actively, as well as undertaking some of the activities listed above.

Using your work experience diary

Your diary is primarily a record of your time in work experience and an invaluable document when you begin preparing for interview questions. This is because referring to your work experience is a good way to demonstrate your commitment to medicine, if you have undertaken it in a proactive, intelligent and thoughtful manner.

Remember that finding the candidate interesting is one of the key selection criteria that admissions tutors are looking for. You can start to select the unique and interesting stories based on patients, doctors and experiences from your placements. I strongly advise against creating stories, as students are often far worse liars than they might think, and it may be difficult to intelligently discuss and reflect upon something that was not a real memory. Further probing of the situation by the interview panel may reveal your lack of a genuine basis. Moreover, if you are applying for a career in medicine, honesty and trustworthiness are key elements in the job, and you should start with your application.

If you have not yet produced a diary, and are preparing for the interview nearer the time, it is still very useful to create a diary. It will help you recall the key points and experiences from your placements and allow you to reflect on how they affected you, your motivation for medicine and your understanding of the profession.

Reviewing your diary before the interview can be a double-edged sword. On the one hand, you may remember the stories freshly in your mind. On the down side, you may end up sounding over-rehearsed, particularly if you write your diary out as if you are designing a speech to be delivered on stage. Write down key facts only to help you cover the material quickly and leave flexibility for you to shape telling the story in your own, natural voice.

Questions

The above section should have given you the raw materials to approach any question related to work experience if you have worked on your diary diligently.

22. Can you tell me about your work experience?

This question is one of the most common faced by students, so to stand out you can use the DPT framework to maximize the interest of your story and add in elements of personal reflection.

Points to consider

Topics to discuss include:

- your experiences of life as a doctor;

- the working environment;

- the training involved;

- the multidisciplinary team;

- your interactions with patients.

Anecdotes focused around medical staff or patients might be the most appropriate when considering experiences with a view to a career in medicine.

Example answer

'One of the main experiences that I have gained insight from is talking to practising doctors. I got to do this most on my work experience attachment at the rheumatology department at Addenbrooke's Hospital. One of the most valuable encounters was with the respiratory medicine team, when I attended a team presentation, and at the subsequent lunch I was able to speak to all the different grades of doctors from F1 to consultant. Each one had their own spin on what they enjoyed about the job – for the F1, she focused very much on day-to-day interactions with patients and making sure that nothing was missed. I felt like I had some things in common with her as part of me has an element of a perfectionist personality. However, it was interesting to contrast this with the consultant, who enjoys undertaking research and working on protocols of treatment of severe asthma, as well as teaching. What I learned from this is that there are many elements of the job that doctors enjoy, and the focus may change during the course of the career, which appeals to me by adding variety to the job. However, the fundamental love of treating patients remains the same and I look forward to the opportunity to enjoy my working life in the same way as all the members of the respiratory team.'

This example answer uses the DPT framework as follows:

- Explain the theory – talking to doctors gave the student insight into medicine.

- Report the event – the insight was gained during work experience in the rheumatology department.

- Manifest (give an example) – the student attended the respiratory medicine team's presentation and lunch.

- Maintain interest with a unique perspective – the student was able to talk to all the different grades of doctor in one meeting.

- Reflect – the student mentions the parts of the job he or she enjoyed.

- Conclude – a patient-focused conclusion is given.

Follow-up

There are several antagonistic (a-chain) follow-ons, one of which might be 'What are the negative sides of being a doctor' (See question 72 for a worked example of a-chain navigation regarding the negative sides.)

23. What was the most challenging aspect of your work experience?

This question can be difficult to answer if you have not considered it beforehand. Usually work experiences do not allow you to participate actively in patient treatment or assessment on the wards, for safety reasons. Therefore, any tasks you will have done will usually be administrative, or helping with logistics, and therefore not hugely challenging; having trouble finding different types of forms on the ward is **not** a great challenge.

Challenges faced by doctors

It might be helpful to discuss some of the issues that you saw other doctors encounter. For example, challenging situations can include breaking bad news to patients, such as serious diagnoses or poor prognoses. Dealing with angry, violent, upset or demanding patients can also be a challenge and reflecting on such things will show that you are looking ahead to your future career and practice. Dealing with problems between colleagues can also be challenging and confrontations at work are another problem you could discuss.

Challenges of the environment

You may also be able to reflect on some personal experiences of the ward environment. You may find it difficult to spend most of your day around sick people, or the smell of urine or faeces that is common on many wards. You may find the sight of blood disturbing, or if you are lucky enough to spend some time in operating theatres you may find it difficult to deal with seeing the human body in this way. Remember to approach this in a balanced way, as you will be working in this environment in the future. You may have found these conditions difficult at first, but later you may have become accustomed to them, which you can comment on in your interview.

Personal challenges

You may have experienced some difficulties, such as keeping up with the ward round, or knowing where to stand when the doctors were attending patients. You may have forgotten to wash your hands or use the alcohol gel to cleanse them when walking in between bays in the ward. You can comment on how you learned as you went along, which may help to show your willingness to learn and adapt.

Conclusion

When you tackle the question, ensure that you put forward a balanced conclusion, as even though these aspects are challenging, other doctors manage to cope with them, and with training and experience you will be able to as well. No job has perfect working conditions, but use this opportunity to express your realistic yet optimistic view of medicine.

Learning task

Ask all members of staff, including nurses, doctors, health care assistants, physiotherapists, pharmacists and occupational therapists, if there is anything you can do to help out. This might give you more active tasks to perform and more to discuss in terms of problems that you found on the wards.

24. In your work experience, what skills have you learned that you can apply to medicine?

Here are some examples:

● Personal attribute framework. You can focus on some key characteristics of doctors who you saw in your placement. It will be helpful if you can refer back to your work experience diary for these, so ensure that you make an effort to record any particularly excellent (or terrible) doctors and what made you think this of them.

- Leadership. Did you see good examples of leadership?

- Teamwork. Did you feel like part of the team? Did you offer to perform simple tasks like pulling the curtain around each patient bay when the team went in to maintain the patient's privacy?

- Communication skills. Did you enjoy talking to patients? Did you find a way to interact with various types of patients?

- Empathy. How did you feel about seeing patients who were ill? Did you take time to talk to them and understand their problems and feelings?

- Commitment. Were you able to maintain your interest and enthusiasm throughout your experience?

Example answer

'One of most valuable skills I started to develop on my work experience was communicating with patients. One of the junior doctors taught me about the basic information he would like to gather from patients, such as their symptoms, eating, drinking, urinary and bowel habits, as well as what medical conditions they had and what medicines they were taking. He sent me to talk to some of the patients and report back to him and I found it was a great experience in learning how to ask questions. I think I started off being like an inquisitor, but I found later on that the best way was to talk to the patients like a normal person and let the information come out in due course rather than forcing it. I found this much more enjoyable as well as informative and I look forward to developing these skills at medical school and in my career.'

25. If you were in charge of the hospital, what would you change or do differently in terms of the ward environment?

This question places you in a difficult position as a student; your work experience may have only lasted days or weeks, and yet it is asking you try and improve on the system that has been set in place by experienced hospital managers and staff. Before you try to do a better job than they are, try the following learning task.

Learning task

One of the best ways of gathering information to help answer this question is to ask the staff working on the wards about what they see as the problems and what they would like to change. You may find it helpful to ask many different types of staff, including all grades of doctors, nurses, health care assistants and administration staff. Don't forget to write down their answers, as you may be able to quote them in your answer. This way, you can draw upon the experiences of others and supplement these with your own ideas.

Example answer

This answer focuses on the answering of hospital phones.

> 'Often the phone on the ward rang and the person who answers it is "selected" at random from whoever is nearby. As a student I would often answer the phone and then set off to track down the relevant person who was being asked for. Both nurses and doctors I have spoken to have considered this a problem and some have said that the phone is such a source of work that they would like to have a staff position just to answer the calls and direct them to the appropriate place. This is one possible solution, and in the future it might be manageable to have some kind of personal communication device for staff members. Doctors may be able to use a hands-free set-up so that they can answer bleeps on the move, or while holding or taking notes. The integration of IT may allow voice recognition in the hospital switchboard and so allow a higher and faster volume of calls to be processed.'

Points to note

This answer touches upon a real problem that hospital doctors will have been subjected to during their working life, demonstrating insight and observational skills from the student. The answer highlights the student's motivation to communicate with the medical team about real day-to-day problems and learn about some of the negative sides of hospital life. It also offers an innovative and forward-looking (if expensive) solution to it.

Some possible problems include:

- low staffing levels;

- insufficient use of electronic technology to replace paper notes;

- poor privacy for patients – the use of curtains to block vision but not sound so that other patients in the bay can easily hear what problems the patient is having;

- hospital-acquired infections such as MRSA or C. difficile.

26. What impressed you most about the doctors in your work experience?

This question tests what you consider to be important characteristics in a doctor, as well as your observational skills on your placement. As usual, it is vitally important that you maintain the interest of the interview panel with an answer that is different from the usual answers to this very common question, by using DPT. You will be able to use your work experience diary directly to answer this question. Read through and find examples of doctors who displayed exceptional prowess in some or all of the following characteristics:

- academic ability;

- communication skills;

- empathy;

- teamwork;

- leadership;

- commitment;

- honesty.

Here is an example DPT-based answer:

- Explain the theory – 'The doctors who impressed me were not so much the ones who had a singular outstanding characteristic such as high intelligence, or exceptional communicators, as much as those who had a combination of many admirable traits.'

- Manifest (give an example) – 'The one doctor who embodied this the most was the surgical registrar (ST 4) on my team. I thought that I would get on best with the junior doctors as they are closest to my age, but the ones on my team seemed quite preoccupied with filling in paperwork and did not have that much time to talk to me, which was understandable. The registrar, on the other hand, seemed experienced enough to manage his workload as well as taking time to teach me things on the ward.'

- Maintain interest with a unique perspective – 'He also managed to keep up a side hobby in rock climbing and was telling me about a recent trip to climb a shore cliff in the South of France.'

- Reflect – 'I really felt that he was a well-balanced individual who did a great job but also enjoyed his work and life in general.'

- Conclude – 'I think the best part of the experience was seeing in real time the combination of great communication skills, teaching ability and just simple friendliness. It's nice to have a role model to work towards in the pursuit of my career in medicine.'

27. Can you tell me the key things you learned from your work experience?

Key learning points

These might include:

- a realistic perspective of medicine as a career;
- insight into the day-to-day life of a doctor;
- advantages and disadvantages of the job;
- the working environment;
- the other members of the health care team.

For each of these learning points consider what you have learned from your experience and discuss them in answer to this question.

Example answer

'One of the things I saw during my work experience was the role that job satisfaction plays in the life of a doctor. The rewards manifest themselves relatively quickly – for example a patient may come in with some abdominal pain, go for surgery and then recover within a few days in the case of appendicitis. The dual rewards of the gratitude of the patient and the professional satisfaction of a job well done both occur quickly. In other jobs, such as directing a feature film or designing a building, this may take many months or even years to occur, and this may be disheartening. I am looking forward to experiencing this kind of working environment in the future, and for both myself and the doctors I have met, it seems to make a large impact on their day-to-day lives.'

It can be helpful if you have had experience of another type of work, for example office-based work, laboratory-based work or employment of another kind, so that you can draw direct comparisons with the life of a doctor. However, you may still draw comparisons to other careers theoretically, for example in the answer to question 28.

28. What did you learn from your voluntary work?

This question is similar to question 27 and you should use a similar approach to design a DPT-based answer to give a reasoned, supported and interesting answer from your experience. You may wish to focus on one of the learning points below.

Learning points from voluntary work include:

- Communication skills – you may have to interact with many different demographics of people.

- Responsibility – you will have tasks to undertake and be expected to complete them well and enthusiastically. You will be expected to turn up on time and regularly.

- Empathy – you may have a better understanding of the people you work with and the problems they face, by spending time with them and talking to them.

- Commitment – a long-term undertaking with voluntary work can give the rewards of getting to know the people you are helping and interacting with. It also shows that you have the ability to commit to an endeavour and see it through for a substantial period.

29. Why do people volunteer?

This question is more concerned with the theory of compassion rather than looking at a specific activity that you have undertaken. Therefore, one approach may be to discuss volunteering in general before going on to discuss any of your experiences.
Some of the benefits of volunteering include:

- learning to interact with various demographics of people;

- learning to manage positions of responsibility;

- personal development;

- improving communication skills;

- acquiring other practical skills or experience, such as teaching;

- increased activity or exercise;

- enhancing a CV;

- public relations benefit.

Consider these questions: Is the motivation more important than the result? If someone volunteers for a non-selfless reason, does this make the person's voluntary work any less meaningful or valid? Volunteering could be a function of practicalities; people could be more likely to volunteer if they have available free time, if it is an activity that they are interested in performing and is convenient for them in terms of timing and location.

30. Is there such a thing as a selfless good deed; do people do things because they truly want to help others, or just to feel better about themselves?

You may wish to consider the following:

- Doing good deeds often results in rewards such as feeling better about oneself and a helpful and kind public image. Therefore, it can be difficult to be sure that this is not the main motivation for doing them.

- Some religions advocate doing good deeds. They may claim that there are rewards or judgement in the afterlife related to these good deeds. You could therefore argue that they are doing good deeds out of duty, seeking of a reward or fear of a punishment, rather than it being entirely selfless.

- Economists may argue that people act in their own interest to maximize their 'utility' and therefore undertake good deeds when it serves their own ends. They may also say that this is the optimal for a system as it incentivizes people to pursue the things they want, rather than them being allocated to them.

- One example of a selfless good deed is doing something good for a person who you dislike. In this way, you do not gain the feeling of reward. However, some psychologists may argue that the motivation for doing the deed may be relief of guilt regarding your dislike of the person.

- Even if it is true that there is no such thing as a selfless good deed, it does not diminish the value of the deeds. If people are able to help themselves and another person at the same time, this might be an ideal situation.

Summary

- Reflecting on your experiences, not simply reporting them or writing them down, is the key to success in these types of question.

- You will find your work experience diary a valuable asset in preparation for interview.

- Ensure that your diary is not a fully written script of what to say, but contains key information and your own reflections, which you can adapt to many types of questions.

- Remember to use DPT where appropriate to enhance your answers.

CHAPTER 6

Personal attributes

Which attributes?

There are many personal attributes that are desirable in a doctor and it is considered important for potential future doctors to understand what they are, and why they are important for the study and practice of medicine.

A number of discussions with admissions tutors have revealed the main attributes that are universally considered to be a prerequisite for doctors and medical students. These are described and explained in the relevant questions pertaining to each attribute. The attributes are:

- teamwork;
- leadership;
- communication skills;
- empathy and compassion;
- commitment and dedication;
- ability to cope with stress;
- honesty.

Attributes and the personal statement

You may have touched on these in your personal statement individually, backing them up with evidence to show that you have, for example, good communication skills. Admissions tutors may wish to explore these statements further by probing with questions pertaining to your listed activity. In particular, they may challenge the links that you have made between the activity and the personal attribute; for example, if you were the captain of a school sports team, they might ask for examples of when you exhibited leadership or what situations required leadership. This line of questioning might then move on to encompass the theory of leadership and your understanding of it.

You must know your personal statement inside out and back to front. Not only must you know the hobbies, interests and extra-curricular activities that you have mentioned, but you must remember what personal attributes you linked them with. You should have a good understanding of exactly what each attribute means, and most importantly, have more to say about each example than what you wrote down on the UCAS personal statement.

The best way to do this is to reflect on your participation, role and interaction with others and on the learning experiences from your activities. You can then write down useful anecdotes, memories and your thoughts on them, ready for the interview. You can use DPT to construct interesting and thoughtful examples of particular events that occurred during the engagement of your activities.

The types of question you may be asked regarding the general attributes of a doctor or on the specific attributes are listed below.

General questions

31. What attributes do you think a good doctor should have?

Consider the following points.

You may wish to comment on the attributes listed above: teamwork, leadership, compassion or empathy, commitment or dedication, communication skills, ability to cope with stress, and honesty. It would probably be too long an answer to discuss the definitions for each of these attributes in full detail. You can mention a clinical context for each one, however; for example 'Teamwork, as a doctor has to play a role as part of a multidisciplinary health care team.'

This question will usually be followed up by asking you to comment on a particular attribute that you have mentioned, so be prepared.

32. Can you tell me about your hobbies?

The interviewers will have your UCAS form in front of them, and this question is often used by admissions tutors to test the integrity of your personal statement.

Maintaining excellent academic achievement while pursuing a hobby can be evidence of good time management, but if your hobbies are leaving you stretched at school, admissions tutors may reasonably extrapolate that this will continue at university. Some hobbies, for example swinging on a hammock sipping pina coladas, can be considered worthless, but most activities, even unusual ones, are usefully included in your personal statement.

It is important you discuss the hobbies you have written about. It would be unusual for you to have a deep passion for an activity, but fail to mention it at all in your personal statement. Avoid making sweeping superficial lists and lead with the hobby you are genuinely most enthusiastic about.

Other interests you might list include things such as music and sports. In order to differentiate between a genuine interest and a superficial one, interviewers may probe deeper into your knowledge of the interest. This is a good diagnostic test and most people who do not have a strong interest will find it hard to express clear favourites, or explain why they like their interest over other similar activities, for example why football rather than basketball. A weak candidate might answer 'I just prefer it', whereas stronger candidates will have a balanced and multifactorial response, for example 'I prefer outdoor sports, and also football has more of a team focus, whereas basketball is more of an individual sport, particularly on offence.'

Avoid making things out to be more than they are, and linking very non-medical things to medicine. For example, if you play badminton, you could, with difficulty, link it to scientific interest by discussing the unique nature of the flight of a shuttlecock that has a parabolic trajectory and adds an interesting dimension to the game, based on physics. However, admissions tutors will be satisfied that you take part in and enjoy activities simply because you like them and that not everything you take part in will be directly relevant to a future career as a doctor. Rather than counting against you, such activities make your character appear deeper and more interesting than that of someone who only discusses medical matters.

Learning task

Ask real cricket enthusiasts about why they enjoy watching test match cricket. It will be helpful to see why they like the sport (which can be rather confusing if you are not a fan), and note down the methods and terminology that they use to convince you of its interest.

33. What are your interests?

Remember that interests and hobbies are different. Interests are the subject or activity that you find stimulating or curious. Hobbies are the manifestation of that interest into an endeavour. Therefore, if you are asked about your interests, it is better to comment more on the intellectual level first, before going on to how you have manifested this interest. For example:

> 'I am fascinated by human interactions and the models that people have created to try to explain and predict these behaviours. I have enjoyed reading books such as Freakonomics and Mystery Method. Although they consider rather unusual subject matter, the way they approach it is quite scientific. Mystery Method is about a man who creates a model for humans flirting in various situation, for example nightclubs. He discusses the biological drives for reproduction and how they have changed from our hunter-gatherer days to modern times, and his observational data on human patterns. I find this approach similar to that of an experimental scientist, observing events, creating hypotheses and testing theories. Freakonomics takes a similar approach, but rather than using biology and behavioural sciences, the author uses economics to explain why interesting events occur, such as teachers encouraging students to cheat in certain schools, or certain names being used predominantly by particular socio-economic groups. I also find the books immensely entertaining, and I very much enjoy the combination of this scientific approach coupled with engaging stories.'

34. What have you accomplished?

This question gives you an opportunity to summarize your key achievements whilst not boring your interviewers with an exhaustive list. You can use the rule of threes to keep the answer at an appropriate length and you may wish to end on your strongest point.

Example answer

> 'I see my main accomplishments as being in three key areas: in academia I have achieved top grades in my examinations, as well as a passing a university level module "Human Genetics" in my own time; in community actions as being a two-year ongoing commitment with a residential home; and in music I have achieved a grade 8 in piano, leading to a charity recital in my local shopping centre to raise money for Cancer Research UK.'

This approach will generate a balanced and impressive impression, whilst opening up several corridors for the interview panel to explore with you, and is another example of c-chain manipulation.

35. What would you like to change about yourself, and why?

A common answer to this question is perfectionism. This is fast becoming the cliché answer to all 'personal fault' type questions as it seems to be a laudable problem to have.

Example answer

'One thing I would say about myself is that I am a bit of a perfectionist. I would like to be able to not have flaws in my work, and I can spend far too much time ironing out small details. However, I do realize that this can become an unhealthy habit bordering on obsession and if I were to change this trait I believe it will enable me to strike a better work–life balance, based on what I have seen and in talking to doctors one to one. Particularly in the GP setting, as well as in psychiatry, patients are allowed to go home without having a definitive diagnosis and are followed up by watchful waiting. In psychiatry, you may make a diagnosis and consider patients safe, but they may go on to harm themselves or others. I think it would be easier to deal with the uncertainties of a medical career if I could move away from this perfectionist streak and learn to tolerate a degree of uncertainty in situations that are not controllable. I suspect this will take both effort on my part as well as some increase in maturity, which I hope to undergo at medical school and in my career beyond.'

Other options students have considered include:

- taking on too much responsibility;
- wanting to help others at the expense of yourself;
- workaholic traits.

You may wish to avoid mentioning purely negative traits such as laziness, selfishness or a poor memory, as it would be hard to see the 'silver lining' in these particular clouds.

36. What qualities do you most need to develop in yourself?

This question requires you to have in-depth knowledge of the qualities required as a doctor, as well as requiring you to select one or two qualities for discussion. Refer to the 'Attributes of a doctor' list on page 77.

Try to focus on one or two qualities which you have some, but not a fully satisfactory level in. For example, you may have some experience in teamwork in sports teams, but you may reflect that you wish to have more teamworking experience, particularly in empathetic or academic pursuits.

> Avoid discussing qualities that are not relevant for your medical application. You may need to develop your ability to remain awake during feature films, or spacial awareness for football games, but these will not aid your bid to gain a place at medical school.

37. How do you think other people would describe you, and how would you like them to describe you?

You may wish to consider the following qualities in your answer:

- honest/genuine/sincere;

- hardworking;

- sympathetic/empathetic/kind;

- intelligent/analytical;

- a team player/inspirational leader.

> Try to include one or two personal items, to give you a human element. For example, saying you wish to be described as humorous may not be directly relevant to life as a doctor (although laughter is the best medicine according to some), but adds a realistic and personal touch to your answer.

38. Can you tell us about someone who has been a major influence on you as a person?

> Describe the person and reflect on how his or her influence has affected you in the past and present and how you think it will do so in the future.

The common answers for candidates include parents, teachers, doctors, friends or peers, but can include more exotic answers such as famous scientists, philosophers or even celebrities. All of these are acceptable as long as you can justify in an intelligent manner why the person has been an influence on you.

39. Which of your hobbies and interests do you think you will continue at university?

It is impossible to cover all the possible answers that candidates will have for this question. However, you should consider carefully which hobbies and interests you intend to continue and phrase the answer to take into consideration the academic commitments you will have on the course. Do research into whether your particular interest has a club or society at the university, and if so, what the standard is. You can use this information to assess critically your ability to reach that level, which can demonstrate humility and rational analysis.

40. Tell us about a film you have seen or book you have read recently that has made you think. Why did it make you think?

Tailor this to the type of course you are applying to. If you are applying to a PBL (problem-based learning) heavy course, you may wish to focus more on communication skills, teamwork, ethics or reasoning, rather than biology or chemistry. You can use this as a chance to demonstrate empathy or understanding of emotion.

If you are applying to Oxbridge, or a science-heavy course, you may wish to focus on a more scientific interest with regard to a book or film. If you are applying to an integrated course, you can use this question to highlight some issues to complement areas that you feel have not been covered by the interview up to that point, either scientific or personal.

In this question almost any book or film can be used, as long as you are able to construct a relevant, coherent and intelligent argument. Be sure to direct the discussion towards aiding your acceptance for a place at medical school, as the panel are not interviewing for a book or film critic position.

Example answer

'I recently watched the film 21, which was about a prospective medical student who is rejected for a scholarship and cannot afford his place, and therefore becomes involved with a mathematics professor to develop algorithms for winning at Blackjack. Although the main character suffered through many hardships as a result, he finally won his place, and I felt it was a wonderful story about the extent to which this student would go to fund his medical degree. As a graduate applicant, I have had to consider to myself many times how much, and how

consistent, my desire to study medicine was, and whilst my life is less dramatic, I can draw parallels in the efforts he made, and my own.'

> In answering this question, you may wish to refer to particular characters, chapters or events, and reflect on what they meant to you as a person.

Teamwork questions

41. Tell us about a time when you were part of a team. What contributions did you make to it?

This question may rely on your extra-curricular activities as the source of the answer. These may include activities associated with:

- sports teams;
- orchestras or choirs;
- society committees;
- youth groups;
- volunteer groups;
- charity events;
- Young Enterprise groups.

> In describing your contributions, you may wish to set the scene by describing what you team's tasks and goals were. It can be helpful to avoid sounding egocentric by describing your role in the context of other roles of your fellow teammates.

42. Can you tell us about a project or group undertaking that you have been involved in?

The ideal situation is that you have a 'flagship' group activity that you are particularly pleased with. In all circumstances, you should not simply describe the activity. Spend some time reflecting on the activity you have undertaken and how it affected you. What did you learn from it? Did it involve teamwork, leadership, communication skills, empathy, compassion and dedication, for example? If so, what did the experience teach you?

Once you have reflected on your activity, it is important to design your answer using DPT. Focus on what elements to highlight. In this case, you could choose between the two events given below.

Planning a group trip

You may have organized a holiday, trip abroad or even a local event. The important skills you can touch on include coordination of tasks and delegating work (leader-ship), choice of medium – e-mail, phone, text, meetings – (communication skills), special considerations of the circumstances of individuals, including concerns such as budget, personal circumstance and mobility (empathy). Use DPT to design an answer that is interesting as well as informative and select a few of these key skill groups to highlight.

You may have taken responsibility for organizing an activity, club, sports team or Duke of Edinburgh Award Scheme expedition at school. It will be particularly helpful if you have been involved in inter-school competitions that require communication and organization with outside agencies.

If none of the above apply, you may wish to consider undertaking some further group activities to enable you to answer such questions.

43. Tell us about a team situation you have experienced. What did you learn about yourself and about successful teamworking?

'Successful teams build camaraderie together. I enjoyed working with and working for people I liked.'

This question is divided into three elements – the first of which is reporting a team-working situation you have been in. This can involve reporting on the event in a concise, interesting manner; be sure to set the scene by describing the task at hand, the team and your role within it.

The second element is describing what you learned about yourself from this ex-perience. Reflective practice is a key element of learning, and you can prepare for such questions by thinking about not only reporting the event, but also how you felt about it. Ask yourself the following questions:

● How did you feel about the activity at the time?

● Looking back on it, what went well and what did you feel went badly?

● How might you have done things differently?

● How will this change your practice in the future?

In answering these questions, you will develop a coherent and concise answer to summarize the reflective learning from your teamworking experience.

The third element is the discussion of teamworking, and discussion of successful teams. You can consider elements such as communication skills, expert knowledge, appropriate delegation of support, camaraderie and team spirit. Be sure not to simply list out these elements, but illustrate them with descriptions of how your team demonstrated these qualities.

44. When you think about yourself working as a doctor, who do you think will be the most important people in the team you will be working with?

Fellow doctors are the first group to consider. Senior doctors will offer guidance, experience and knowledge to help you develop your own skills in diagnosis and management of patients. They will also be there to assist you with patients when your own skills are insufficient. Having junior doctors will allow you to delegate work and also be involved in their training, improving their knowledge while gaining valuable teaching experience yourself. They will also be a source of emotional support as you will be going through similar difficulties as a group.

These members of team will also have an impact on your work:

- nurses;

- administration staff;

- pharmacists;

- allied therapists;

- managers.

45. Who are the important members of a multidisciplinary health care team, and why?

One way to organize your answer to this question is to make it patient-centric, for example as follows:

> 'The members of the multidisciplinary team who are most important depends on the medical and social conditions of the patient. For example, a young patient who had a fracture of the tibia and fibula whom I saw on my work experience in the orthopaedic ward, felt one of the most helpful non-medical members of staff was the physiotherapist who helped him remobilize quickly after his operation. In contrast, for an elderly lady who had fallen and fractured the neck of her femur, both the occupational therapist and social workers were very important in her care. The occupational therapist assessed the patient's ability to cope with day-to-day tasks and made recommendations to make them easier bearing in mind her reduced mobility, and social

workers arranged additional help by having carers visit her at home three times per day to assist with tasks such as washing and dressing, which she was struggling to perform by herself in the ward. Other situations might call for other members of the multidisciplinary team, such as the palliative care team or Macmillan nurses for patients with terminal cancer.'

An answer to question 45 like the one given also allows you to insert additional positive selection triggers, such as in-depth medical knowledge and terminology – in this case fractured tibia and fibula, compared to the fracture of the neck of femur, which is more common in older patients suffering from osteoporosis (so more frequent in females).

Leadership

46. How would you describe a good leader?

You may wish to comment on the following characteristics:

- Ability – a leader may have a high ability to undertake a certain task. This may be academic, as in the knowledge possessed by a consultant leading a medical team. It may be physical prowess in a sports team.

- Organization skills – these may include appropriate delegation of tasks to individuals, as well as planning for activities in general.

- Communication skills – these are vital for conveying the messages and instructions needed to operate a good team.

- Charisma – this is a slightly intangible quality of 'likeability' that leaders may possess. A person may be a talented and organized good communicator, but this does not mean that person will be liked by a team. Characteristics such as a considerate nature and good sense of humour may play an important role in charisma.

47. Are you a leader or a follower?

Example answer

'Being a leader or a follower depends on the situation; I have been both a leader and a follower depending on what the situation calls for. For example, in circumstances where I have been less experienced or accomplished than others, I have been a follower. In my Duke of Edinburgh experience, we all had a similar level of experience in leading expeditions (which is to say, very

little), and so each of us took it in turns to be leader. I would say that I do enjoy leading and the sense of accomplishment that comes with it, for example when I led the fencing team to victory in the district championships. I helped to design the training programme and practice, and also I feel that together with the coach I managed to pull together the team spirit by getting everyone involved, even the juniors, in the fencing events leading up to the tournament and helping to organize the logistics. This led me to feel a great sense of achievement and to enjoy the role of being a leader, along with the responsibility. However, I would say my participation as a leader or follower is dictated by my own abilities, viewed in terms of the needs of the group.'

It is not necessarily 'better' to be a leader or 'worse' to be a follower. Demonstrate to the interview panel that you understand what it means to be a team player in both roles.

48. What are the advantages and disadvantages of being in a team?

Some of the advantages are as follows:

- responsibility and therefore pressure is spread among several people;
- team members may have different skill sets that complement each other;
- physical and emotional support are available.

Examples of disadvantages include: the performance of other team members can be an uncontrolled variable; and decision-making processes can take longer when carried out by a team than by individuals.

49. Do teams need leaders?

Consider these points for the argument that teams need leaders:

- Leaders are a focal point for representing a team.
- Leaders can provide inspiration as well as organization. This may stem from good communication skills or exceptional prowess at a particular endeavour.
- Decision making is faster when there is an appointed leader and a chain of command.

Here are some points against the argument that teams need leaders. Some teams may function best as a collaboration, which does not require an overall leader, such as artistic collaborations. Leadership may be gained from having several leaders for subsections of a team, which can be more helpful than having a single leader.

Communication skills

50. Think of a situation when communication skills have been important. Can you tell us about what happened?

You may wish to consider the following situations:

- Classroom communication – this can be between students collaborating on a piece of work, or teacher–student communications.

- Public communication – this could involve an everyday occurrence such as a customer arguing with a shop assistant, or an emergency situation.

- Activity-based communication – this could be between teammates of a sports team, fellow members of a society, or even musical communication as part of a jazz band.

> The use of DPT will allow you to create an anecdote to illustrate the communication situation, as well as showcasing your own verbal communication skills by maintaining the interest of the panel.

51. Can you learn communication skills?

Avoid answers such as 'No, I think people are born with good communication skills.' Medical schools have a number of methods of teaching communication skills to students, including lectures and practice with actors pretending to be patients with real diseases. This allows the student to learn the principles of effective communication. For examples of people who need to be effective in communicating ideas to people clearly, and enabling them to respond, you could draw upon the examples of actors or politicians.

52. How have you developed your communication skills?

Consider the following in your answer:

- You may have had formal coaching in a branch of communication, such as acting, singing or debating. This is certainly worth mentioning as it is an objective method of improving verbal communication.

- Experiential learning may form an important part of the development of your communication skills. This can include presentations, public speaking or listening to teams.

- Learning to communicate with people in different age groups can be gained from voluntary work or work experience.

53. What skills do you think are needed in order to communicate with your patients?

This question can be answered by referring to the preparation section of the book (Chapter 1). You may wish to refer to communication as an input (listening to the patient), a process (integrating the data with your own knowledge and experience) and an output (communicating back to the patient clearly).

Empathy and compassion

54. What is empathy?

Empathy involves the ability to share the feelings of another person, and plays an important role in the communication and relating of humans to one another. Being an empathetic listener, for example, can be helpful in medicine and can be expressed by both verbal and non-verbal cues. However, the 'empathy' element is in listening to the content of the speaker and understanding what emotions they are going through.

Example answer

'Empathy is the process of sharing the emotions of another human being, for example, when a doctor breaks the news of a death of a patient to a relative, he might be able to empathize with this experience, thereby relating this to his own experiences, and this can allow him to comfort the patient in some way.'

In answering interview questions, try to utilize the opportunity to give medical examples to demonstrate your understanding of the career.

55. Are you a compassionate person?

This question is a difficult one to answer, precisely because compassion is difficult to measure, and the question challenges you to prove that you are. Compassion is considered a key quality in medical selection, as the motivation to help people is often one that encourages academically gifted students to choose medicine over another, more theoretical application of their scientific knowledge, and therefore it is important to consider how compassionate you are, and how you might best illustrate this.

Consider the following activities to refer to:

- voluntary work;

- helping a schoolmate with work;

- organizing charity events;

- helping people on the street;

- assisting family or friends, for example taking care of a sick relative.

It may be helpful to recall some particular events or activities that you have undertaken that demonstrate compassion, but are not necessarily formalized into an achievement, certificate or other activity. This will give a unique approach to dealing with a characteristic that can be difficult to assess objectively.

Commitment and dedication

56. The study of medicine requires considerable commitment. What can you tell us about yourself that shows you have this commitment?

This question has the prerequisite not only that you understand the theory of commitment and dedication, but also that you are able to draw on experiences from your own life. It is therefore more difficult to answer if you have not had any long-term commitments in terms of extra-curricular activities.

Use examples of commitment such as:

- a long-standing effort in a particular academic pursuit;

- regular attendance at a society or club;

- an event where you went beyond what was expected of you, for a cause, for example working all night immediately before the publication of a school newspaper was due to write a section for a sick colleague;

- achievement or participation in an extra-curricular activity, while maintaining high academic scores.

57. Can you give us an example of when you demonstrated dedication?

This question is similar to the previous one, but asks you for a specific event, occasion, activity or pursuit that demonstrates this quality. You can use examples of activities from the previous question.

> DPT is most useful for questions asking for an individual example, as using all the elements of the framework will allow you to give a sizeable, substantive as well as unique answer.

Ability to cope with stress

58. How do you cope with stress?

Stress can be caused by a build-up of pressure of things to do. Therefore using the commonest answer, which is to say that you are going to cope with stress simply by relaxing and unwinding, does not adequately deal with the problem of a huge 'to do' list; rather it compounds it by taking up your time. A better strategy would be to use organization skills to compartmentalize these tasks into groups, and then prioritizing.

Goal setting is very important, and one tool that is often used is SMART goals, that is to say Specific, Measurable, Achievable, Realistic and Time-constrained goals. Thus, the standard answer to 'relaxing with music' might be useful in rewarding yourself after you have achieved each short-term goal, giving yourself an incentive to work towards them and also a well-deserved break to allow you to rest.

Prevention is better than cure, which means not allowing things to build up. Being aware of fluctuations in your own mood due to tiredness, hormonal change or weather can help to at least prepare yourself, and others around you, for periods of stress and help you to navigate them easily.

> Parkinson's law states that work expands or contracts to fill the time allocated for its completion. Therefore, you could state that you could use this law by constraining your work to time slots in order to maximize efficiency.
>
> However, note that Parkinson's law only holds to an elastic limit, after which the work cannot be fitted into too small a time frame.

Honesty

59. Should a doctor be honest at all times?

Example answer

'I would say that a doctor should be honest in general, but may be dishonest under specific circumstances. A doctor is also a person and therefore subject to the general ethical principles regarding honesty. The golden rule states that you should do unto others as you would want to be done by. The principle of autonomy states that we are best respecting a person's choice by giving them all the information to make decisions, which involves honesty.

Utilitarianism ethics searches for the greatest good for the greatest number. Therefore, in economic terms, it is optimal for a monetary system if people are honest – such that in a simple interaction between a buyer and a seller, business can occur more readily if a seller is sure that the buyer will pay on time, and the buyer is sure that the product will do as it is advertised, and people are more likely to make trades and stimulate the economy. This system breaks down if there is fear of deception, and may incur more costs, such as hiring a third party to ensure that the trade is fair.

A doctor's relationship with a patient can be similar to this economic trade, but with certain additional constraints. The patient may have to tell the doctor information that the patient feels is private or embarrassing, in order for the doctor to make a more accurate diagnosis. The patient is therefore more likely to volunteer this information if the doctor is honest and confidential, which in turn would make the doctor's job more efficient and allow the patient benefits from better treatment. Therefore, it is in the interests of both the patient and doctor for them to be honest.

However, deception can play an important role in medicine. The placebo effect of medication relies upon the deception that an inert substance will have a healing effect, and may result in perceived and real benefits. It requires the patient to think that the medication will work, when it doesn't, and therefore cannot work if a doctor is honest about it. Thus I think a doctor should generally be honest in life and with patient interactions. However, there are specific instances where deception may be justified in the greater interest of the patient.'

Additional considerations and examples

A proportion of medical trial subjects are 'deceived' as they can be given a placebo medication. However, since they are usually informed at the beginning of the trial that this would be a possibility, they are given some statistical information regarding their treatment, and the doctors are also 'blinded' as to who is having a placebo or not (to prevent bias) and so doctors are not actively deceiving the individuals as they also do not know.

One consideration is the legal principle of therapeutic privilege, which states that a doctor may withhold information, such as a diagnosis, if there is a risk of real and predictable harm resulting from imparting the information. This may occur, for example, when a doctor is deciding whether or not to inform a patient with depression about a severe diagnosis that may put the patient at a higher risk of suicide. This balances the principles of non-maleficence and beneficence, as usually deception is associated with causing harm, but in these cases the deception is for preventing harm.

Summary

- This chapter contains a vast amount of information which you can put to good use in answering personal attribute questions, and may need reviewing several times before interview.

- It is important to understand the means of the attributes you are describing, such as empathy or teamwork.

- This chapter also lends itself well to the use of DPT, as answers often involve an anecdote of your own life.

- Practise, practise and practise making your stories interesting and compelling.

CHAPTER 7

Knowledge of the medical school

Introduction

There is a difference in opinion on what constitutes the best method for medical education. Traditional, integrated and PBL methods form the main basis for the divide. However, there are also variations in the amount of 'student-selected' components versus 'core' curricular content. Methods for teaching communications skills involve various proportions of seminars and workshops where students interact with actors in simulated clinical conditions that can safely replicate situations such as dealing with angry and upset patients.

Medical schools are quite rightly proud of their individual curricula and teaching styles. It is important to get to know not only your school of choice's method, but also what the other possibilities are, so that interviewers can be more assured that you have considered the options and come to a balanced decision on their medical school, rather than stumbling on it by chance.

Moreover, it is essential for you to spend the time and effort to select your destination for the next five or six years carefully. This will make the difference between you enjoying your time and thriving at university and beyond, or finding yourself struggling on a course that is not very suitable for you.

The important information that you should know about each course you are applying for includes the following:

- Teaching style – broadly this will be traditional, integrated or PBL.

- Length of course – this will typically be five years, graduate courses may last four years and mandatory intercalated courses take six years.

- Intercalation policy – this involves taking an additional year of in-depth study, which may include research. You will need to know whether intercalation is mandatory (Oxbridge) or selective.

- Patient contact – how early does this occur?

- Dissection – does your teaching of anatomy involve the dissection of a human cadaver?

- Hospital placements – will you be placed in a district hospital, a central teaching hospital or a combination of the two?

- Elective – this is a period of time, usually between four and eight weeks, where you can undertake a placement of your choice, usually abroad. It is used by students to explore an area of their interest, such as trauma and orthopaedics in South Africa or working with the flying doctors in Australia.

- Student-selected components – these are components in the course that can be selected by students to suit their own particular interests or learning needs. They often cover an element of research or specialized clinical experience. Many medical schools also offer some non-medical components, such as the history of medicine, or languages.

- Communication skills.

- Clinical skills – how practical skills, such as taking blood from patients and placing catheters, are covered.

This may seem like a vast amount of information to find out; and furthermore it may not all be instantly available on a single page. You may need to search thoroughly through the medical school's website, and enquire at the offices or ask current students if things are not clear. However, bear in mind that you should really review this information when you are making your decision on which medical school to apply for. It will give you a better idea of the type of teaching and experience you are likely to get and when clinical experience will become a feature in the training. You will only have to retain the details of four medical schools (the current maximum you can apply to under UCAS) for the interview.

Questions

60. What interests you about the course at this medical school?

This question is an open one and invites you to highlight areas of the course that you think are particularly appealing. This necessitates not only knowing what the course entails, but also knowing the nature of other courses so that you can compare and contrast, and reason why you are specifically interested in the medical school in question. Testing your overall knowledge of the course is also a good way to see if you have made a thorough effort in research for your medical school application.

You can use this as an opportunity to steer the conversation towards topics that you are comfortable speaking about. You will need to apply a different answer depending on which type of medical school you are applying to. There is little point in talking about self-directed learning, problems-based approach and independent study in a course that focuses heavily on didactic teaching methods, tutorials and lectures.

General course highlights may include the following.

The elective and student-selected components

You may wish to experience how medicine works abroad. Most medical school have an elective, so it is not a unique feature of a course by any means. However, some medical schools have the electives after the final examinations so that you will be free of pressure to enjoy learning medicine in a practical manner. Other medical schools have it before finals so that you can gain more clinical exposure that will help you in your examinations.

Some medical schools will allow student-selected components in other, non-medically-specific subjects, for example languages or history. You can comment on this, although remember that you are applying for a medical course primarily and you should make it clear that your interests in other subjects are very much secondary.

Intercalation

Taking an intercalated degree involves undertaking an in-depth study into a subject of your choice, leading to the award of an additional degree such as a Bachelor of Science. Find out what subjects might interest you, which will aid your discussion at interview and demonstrate your eagerness.

PBL

For a **PBL medical school**, specific course highlights may include the following elements.

There may be a self-directed learning element. PBL teaching is described in later questions, but essentially involves learning from materials surrounding a clinical case that is self-directed by the student. Therefore, if you enjoy independent and group learning, you can discuss this in your answer. Another aspect is that on a PBL course, you will have freedom to practise time management.

There is often early exposure to patients on PBL courses, and you may be eager to see patients. Try to tie this in to your work experiences.

For a **traditional medical school**, you may wish to focus on discussion of teaching methods such as tutorials, essay writing and research, and comparing these will complement your own work ethic of independent study.

For an **integrated medical school**, you may wish to comment on striking a balance between the fully independent learning of the PBL style, and the didactic teaching at traditional schools, and finding an optional balance in your approach to acquiring a medical knowledge base.

Consider referring to specific elements in the course, eg anatomy dissection, laboratory experiments or the opportunity to undertake research.

Research is a key element of preparing this question, and it is helpful to talk to current students in the medical school.

61. Why did you choose this medical school?

This question is more open than the ones that address only one aspect of the medical school, such as the course itself. Therefore, in addition, you could raise the following issues.

Geography

This may be a factor for any of these reasons:

- You want to stay living near to home for some particular reason.

- You wish to experience living in another part of the UK.

- You want to see a different patient demographic, for example larger cities may see a wider variety of patients, possibly with more ethnic diversity.

- Large teaching hospitals may offer specialist treatments, such as shock wave therapy for kidney stones, or deep brain stimulation for epilepsy.

Facilities

There may be particular facilities that have attracted you to the medical school in question.

Tradition or reputation

Your selection of a particular medical school may be based on the national or international reputation of the standard of teaching or research at this institution. You may wish to refer to this in your answer but try to have some factual basis for it, for example quoting a ranking from a well-recognized source, such as *The Times Guide to Good Universities*.

62. What do you know about the course at (... medical school) and why do you think it will suit you personally?

This is similar to question 60, but you should take this opportunity to discuss your own previous learning experiences and achievements. This will again involve a large amount of research and preparation, not only to understand the course, but to relate it to yourself and prepare answers in a prospective manner.

Below are examples of linking information between the course and your experience:

- Laboratory research and your experience of designing practical experiments at A-level.

- Lecture-based teaching and your attendance at a medical talk on diabetes.

- Special study modules and your own interest in alternative medicines.

- PBL learning and your independent study of a short biology course.

63. What do you know about PBL?

PBL encourages students to direct their own studying. Typically, students are given a clinical scenario, such as the following:

> *'Mrs X is a 69-year-old lady who lives on her own in a house with an upstairs bedroom and bathroom. She has a past medical history of asthma, angina and cataracts. Over several weeks, she notices pain in her knee, which causes her difficulty in moving around the house.'*

Students will determine the learning objectives that stem from such clinical scenarios, for example in this case they may wish to explore the range of conditions that can give you a painful knee, for example osteoarthritis. They may explore the social and psychological consequences of impaired movement, and the anatomy of the knee joint.

PBL sessions are attended by a facilitator, usually a member of staff or doctor, who is present to answer any questions and help the students formulate their plans, but will not take part in formal teaching in the traditional sense. The facilitators are therefore not teachers in the usual sense of the term, which students in high school would be used to. In fact, the 'teachers' of a PBL course are the students themselves, as they feed back to one another and teach other members of the group what they have learned through their independent study.

These are the key features of PBL:

- it has a clinical basis;

- it offers significant self-directed learning;

- there are various levels of taught support;

- early patient contact is common in PBL courses.

In answering this question, avoid simply reporting back about PBL. Use the opportunity to reflect on how this course may suit you, and which elements you are most looking forward to.

64. What do you think are the advantages and disadvantages of a PBL course?

One advantage of a PBL course is that PBL integrates medical education and focuses on patient-centric problem-solving approaches, as well as team and independent learning. Another advantage is the flexible timetable, which is particularly helpful for those with many extra-curricular interests, or who prefer to work at certain times in the day. This can lead to a cadence where you end the question on a subject that you feel comfortable talking about, for example, 'Another benefit of PBL is the flexibility it gives me to plan my own schedule, so that in the winter I can do rowing training in the morning and concentrate on studies later in the day.'

There may be disadvantages for some students who are less independently motivated – they may not be suited to a PBL course and would benefit from a more teacher- or lecture-based approach. Another possible disadvantage is that some subjects such as biochemistry and physiology require a considerable amount of understanding and can be difficult to learn from textbooks alone.

65. Why do you want to come to a PBL medical school?

As discussed above, PBL is most beneficial for highly motivated self-studiers. It is therefore important for you not only to declare that this fits your personality, but also to demonstrate that this is the case. This may involve giving examples of activities outside of school such as learning a new language or even skills such as self-taught guitar.

Part of the PBL learning environment is teaching the others in the group about what you have learned, and experience of revision in groups may demonstrate that you are suitable for this. This can be as simple as discussing problems in the school common room or organizing out-of-school revision sessions among friends.

Experience of more formal teaching, for example a Saturday morning programme where you teach science to younger year students, will be valuable here and many of the skills you will pick up will be useful for PBL.

It is helpful to speak to current students of the medical school and relay some of their experiences; this will demonstrate initiative. However, beware of placing too much emphasis on their opinions, as the sample size of students you have spoken to will probably be small and their opinions will definitely not be representative of the student body as a whole.

66. How do you study, and do you think this method will be successful at university?

Try to avoid focusing your efforts on cramming in the last few weeks before examinations. Although it certainly works, the half-life of the information in your brain will be relatively short and you may forget it soon after the examination is over. The best way to produce long-term memory is to develop a keen understanding of the principles involved in the material you are learning. You may then be able to reason the answers to questions from first principles, even if you have forgotten some elements of the facts. In medicine you will have to learn and retain a vast amount of information and demonstrating to examiners that you have the appropriate study skills will help convince them that you are appropriate for the long and difficult course.

You may study in groups with your peers. This can be a useful activity to refer to as it may reflect to some degree the type of learning experience you will have to undertake as part of a PBL course.

Activities may include:

- formal study sessions in groups;

- informal study in groups;

- discussion of syllabus and requirements;

- joint practice-paper sessions.

Outside reading

This may include a variety of sources, such as:

- medical or scientific journals;

- the internet;

- scientific books;

- independently studied courses;

- reading medical guidelines or protocols in a hospital setting;

- lecture notes from medical or scientific lectures.

67. What previous experiences have you had of learning in a small-group setting?

There are several possible experiences you can draw upon. AS-level class sizes may be variable and, depending on your school, your less popular subjects may have few students per class. This may allow you to discuss the differences between the large classes that may be centred on direct teaching, and the smaller classes that may offer more scope for discussion and interaction. You might wish to talk about tuition, group work and school group activities. For example, as part of your school curriculum you may be given a group project to undertake with fellow classmates. This could involve a presentation on a topic for class (or a bigger audience), a large-scale experiment or a field trip including data collection for a communal project.

Consider your experiences of independent work or teamwork. In independent work, students are often more involved in the design or concept of presentations. In teamwork students can be left to allocate the distribution of work among themselves. This may lead to the acquisition of teamworking and negotiation skills in finding who is the most appropriate candidate for different sections of the work.

If it has led to conflict, you can reflect on what went wrong, how it might have been avoided and what you would do in a future similar situation (which you may face at university).

Some schools require the students of a class to give an assembly or presentation in public; this can be a valuable source of discussion.

68. Apart from a medical education, what else will you gain from medical school?

There are several transferable skills that you will acquire at university:

- Communication skills are among the most valuable skills that you will acquire and will be helpful for many other kinds of activities or employment. You will learn how to listen effectively, and give both verbal and non-verbal cues to patients to build up rapport. You will learn a number of formal techniques, such as summarizing and signposting to help the patients to follow the flow of the conversation.

- Analytical skills – as a medical student you will have to integrate information from various sources such as patients' symptoms and signs, as well as test results, to try and establish a diagnosis and treatment plan. This will develop your skills in analysing information.

- Data interpretation.

- Teaching experience – senior medical students can sometimes be involved in teaching.

- Research skills.

Other things that you may gain include:

- maturity;

- opportunities to hold positions of responsibility;

- a general university experience, including interacting with peers from other disciplines and subjects, which may broaden your outlook;

- the possibility to take part in a variety of extra-curricular activities;

- the possibility of international experience on electives or other academic opportunities such as exchange programmes with overseas universities;

- possible employment opportunities.

69. How do you think you will contribute to the medical school?

Several types of answer may be helpful in approaching this question.

Example answer

'First and foremost I will be a medical student, and I expect to do well in my pursuit of medical knowledge, and represent the medical school on electives or other courses at other institutions. I also look forward to getting involved in medical society activities. I hope to carry on playing the violin and I may try to get involved with the university charities society by doing a charity performance. Having looked at the activities and societies list for the university, I am most interested in the rock-climbing society. There are wilderness medicine societies at other universities but as far as I know not at this university, and therefore I hope to combine my academic and extra-curricular interests by forming a society once I have had some experience of university life. I hope this will add to the diversity and richness of the medical school.'

70. Are there any particular hobbies or activities that you hope to pick up at university?

The answer to this question generally falls under two categories: activities that you hope to start fresh in university and have no previous experience of and those that you wish to pursue based on your current or previous hobbies. For example, you may wish to try tango dancing after discussing with a current medical student at the university what she does to relax. You may wish to build on your own sporting experience, by taking up rowing (which was not available at your school) to complement your own interest in rugby.

Example answer

'I have spoken to several medical students who were involved in the annual medically-themed comedy production, which they wrote, produced and directed themselves. This seems like a wonderful opportunity, and something that would appeal to me based on my previous participation in the backstage crew of three school plays, where I developed my experiences starting off as a stage hand, and ending up as the producer of the senior school production. I hope to apply these skills, as well as trying my hand at writing, all with a medical twist that I will be learning here!'

Summary

- It is important to know in detail about the course you are applying for in order to give the impression of diligence and thoroughness in your approach.

- It can be helpful to speak to current students on the course and you can refer to this in your answers to many questions about your knowledge of the medical school.

- If you are applying to a PBL medical school, you should have a good knowledge of the nature, advantages and disadvantages of a PBL-based course.

- When preparing your answers for this section of the interview, consider the advantages and potential experiences available to you at the medical school in question.

CHAPTER 8

Medicine as a profession

Introduction

Medicine is not only an academic pursuit, but a profession as well, with all of the responsibilities and privileges associated with that status. At interview, understanding of a doctor's professional life is often tested by the questions found in this chapter, and this understanding forms an important part of the impression a candidate gives. Admissions tutors have said that although genuine enthusiasm for medicine can sometimes be faked or simulated, knowledge of not only facts but also experiences and understanding of the future profession cannot be easily replicated. This is because the data are not readily available in text books and are usually gained from hospital placements and speaking to doctors. The questions also require an element of personal reflection on the topics. Candidates who answer well have undergone this process and it is often correlated with genuine interest and genuine curiosity.

This chapter gives details of the key questions that are repeatedly asked at interview and provides you with both example answers and factual information that you might find hard to source otherwise. Learning tasks in this chapter are based around gathering knowledge and reflecting on it, so that you are ready to share with the interview panel both the raw data and your personal thoughts on the subject, to give well-considered answers.

Questions

71. What will be the main challenges in your work as a doctor?

Try to answer this question in a way that acknowledges the difficulties of the job, while including references to doctors you have met, or yourself, in how those difficulties might be dealt with.

Example answer

'I think we can divide the challenges into clinical, communication and personal challenges. Clinically, the first challenge will be the long journey to acquire both the knowledge and skills to undertake effective medical practice. On top of this, one challenge may be complicated, difficult patients who present in unusual ways, although this may also be one of the exciting challenges, in figuring out what might be the root of the problem. Understanding that as humans we may make errors in clinical judgement, and dealing with the consequences will be a challenge. One psychiatry consultant I spoke to on my work experience placement said that he was sometimes nervous when he discharged depressed patients in case they committed suicide, but he said that the best way to deal with this anxiety was experience, understanding the statistics that you will probably get it wrong a few times in your life, and taking comfort and advice from colleagues and friends.

In terms of communication, dealing with angry, depressed or unreasonable patients will be a challenge, and I believe there are some formal training programmes in medical schools on how to cope with such situations on the technical side, and also I think again support from peers, seniors and friends may help on the emotional side of this challenge. Communicating with other members of your team and with the health care multidisciplinary team may also be challenging.

Lastly, personal challenges may include coping with the pressure of making important decisions about someone's health, as well as the stresses of a busy job. There may be physical challenges, which I have seen mostly in the junior years as the F1 doctors may have to rush from ward to ward, carry heavy notes and gather equipment for intravenous injections. Striking a work–life balance can also be a challenge, especially when working on-call shifts on weekends and nights. However, several doctors have said that having outside interests and hobbies to relax them and take their minds off work can be very helpful in keeping their motivation going year on year.'

You can stratify the challenges into different types as follows: 'I consider the challenges of a career in medicine as falling into four categories: intellectual, emotional, physical and ethical.'

Intellectual

'The challenge of training to be a doctor involves long years of study, and will require both understanding of important concepts, as well as a good and long-lasting memory. These will only be acquired by putting in years of effort and revising in an intelligent way. I hope to navigate this by taking advice from my seniors and teachers, as well as having a balanced approach to revision. The application of this knowledge on the wards will be the next step, and taking part in lifelong learning and experiences will continue the intellectual challenge.'

Emotional

'There will be many difficult situations to face, the most daunting of which is seeing suffering and loss of life. I think there may also be difficulties with patients who are violent or aggressive, and I'm sure it is difficult at times to put aside our human nature to judge. I hope, however, that experience, help from colleagues and the training itself will equip me to deal with such situations.'

Physical

'Many junior doctors have told me about on-call and night shifts, which can be very physically taxing even though they are in line with the European working time directive overall. Other physical challenges may come from long operations in theatre. In this case I think taking breaks where possible, and having a good work–life balance, may help to ease the stress associated with difficult working conditions.'

Ethical

'There may be several ethical dilemmas that I face as a doctor. Some of the issues I have discussed include consent to treatment, particularly in patients who do not have the capacity to consent for a medical or other reason, and how a doctor must apply the "best interests test" in conjunction with opinions from other members of staff, friends and family to decide on a course of action. Other dilemmas that I could be facing in my career include dealing with abortion, euthanasia and child protection issues.'

Points to note

The example answer to question 71 has several key points that help the candidate to communicate value. It uses cadence to guide the admissions tutors into certain areas, particularly towards an ethics discussion around medical consent. Cadence does not only apply to the end – for example this answer mentioned the on-call shifts that were discussed with junior doctors on work experience, and the candidate might move on to talk about these, or follow on more naturally from the end of the answer into ethical dilemmas, such as 'What is your opinion on euthanasia? What is its legal status in the UK?'

Learning task

Ask the doctors you meet what they do and don't enjoy about their job. Remember to write these down on the same day that you hear them and think about what they have said. Ask yourself, are you really looking forward to these challenges or rewards? Or do they put you off such a career? By reflecting on what you have discussed, you can start to convince yourself that medicine is, or is not, the career for you, and convincing yourself is the first step towards giving a genuine and convincing answer to an interview panel.

72. What do you think will be the positive aspects and the negative aspects of being a doctor?

You may wish to include the following.

Positive aspects

Rewarding work

'I should say in no uncertain terms that the work of a doctor is immensely rewarding. It is a pleasure to be involved in the health care of others, and you feel that you are making a hands-on and active contribution to society. Although the stories that make news headlines often involve disgruntled patients and lawsuits, the day-to-day reality is that most patients and their families are very grateful to the doctors who look after them.'

Human interaction

There are many jobs that involve a great deal of human interaction, and medicine is one of them. In almost every discipline there is a positive need to talk to people on a daily basis, which gives variety and interest. This varies from patients to other doctors, as well as other members of the health care team.

If you enjoy a hands-on career – as one student described it, 'I'd like to be a human body engineer' – then not only is surgery an attractive option, but other branches of medicine are increasingly having procedure-based activity, such as bronchoscopy for respiratory physicians and gastroscopy for gastroenterologists (using flexible optical fibre cameras to investigate the lungs or stomach from the inside).

Defined career path

The current career path is set out by the NHS Modernising Medical Careers team, which gives a degree of predictability in how your training will develop. There are also opportunities for gap years and 'Time Out of Training' for pursuits such as research or to pursue personal goals such as sporting or business endeavours.

The 2014 figures for basic annual salary were around £22,636 for FY1 doctors and £28,076 for FY2 doctors, although these can be increased by up to 50 per cent depending on the hours of work and on-call commitments. ST doctors earn between £37,176 and £69,325, and consultants between £75,249 and £101,451. (Figures taken from NHS careers: www.nhscareers.nhs.uk)

Lifelong learning

Practising medicine requires you to draw on a large body of knowledge on a daily basis. This knowledge base must be kept up to date and accurate, and there are many opportunities in on-the-job training, courses and literature to improve your database of knowledge during your career.

Evidence-based medicine is the practice of using treatments that have been shown to be the most effective in clinical trials. This means that doctors will have to keep up to date with new treatments as well as new studies, in order to give the best patient care. New technology and new procedures are always on the horizon and a career in medicine will never be monotonous.

Disadvantages

Long and difficult training

From the beginning of medical school to becoming a consultant takes a minimum of 13 years of training, many of which are accompanied by examinations. Medical school can be demanding with a high workload. Life as a junior doctor is constantly busy and as you progress in seniority the pressure of critical decision making can be stressful.

Responsibility

Small clerical or numerical errors, such as prescribing the wrong drugs or doses, can cause serious, permanent injury or death to a person under your care. If you are concerned about your ability to be responsible on a day-to-day basis, this a very serious consideration.

As a doctor you will be in a position that may expose you to lawsuits, and the risk of medical negligence or (rarely) manslaughter. Such incidents may end your career and even land you with a jail sentence, depending on the severity of the incidents.

You will also be responsible for your behaviour outside of work, and even relatively minor infractions of the law can have serious consequences. You may be summoned to the General Medical Council (GMC) for a disciplinary hearing.

Geographical instability

At present, the selection system for higher training is very competitive and geographical stability may be difficult. Some doctors have found themselves training in less than familiar locations owing to the national allocation scheme. This scheme allows you to rank deaneries in order of preference and your job is allocated according to score. In essence, it can be difficult for everyone to get training in both the specialty and location of their choice and you may be forced to compromise on one or the other. Such problems are a long way off from those applying to medical school, but are worth considering when thinking about medicine as a career.

Working environment

The dangers of the working environment for doctors include exposure to infectious disease and occupational health problems such as chronic back pain. In addition, doctors are exposed daily to bodily fluids: blood, faeces, urine and lung secretions. Perhaps more importantly, doctors are surrounded by ill patients every working day of their lives. If you have found this an unpleasant or depressing environment during your work experience, do you want to spend the rest of your life working in such conditions? There are some medical specialties that are based more away from patients such as radiology, where you will spend a lot of time looking at images of patients (such as X-rays) rather than patients themselves.

73. Medicine involves a lifelong process of learning, training and keeping up to date. How will you deal with these demands?

A good answer to this question will include a full assessment of the activities that doctors currently undertake in the pursuit of keeping up to date with medical practice. Most students will not be able to comment on 'grand rounds' and e-portfolios as they do not have an understanding of their role in the day-to-day life of a doctor.

The types of activities available for lifelong learning are as follows:

● Hospital departmental meetings – most hospital departments operate a weekly meeting where all the consultants and junior doctors gather together and give talks on evidence-based medicine, interesting cases or departmental guidelines.

- 'Grand rounds' – hospital-wide meetings that all doctors are required to attend, usually for a half day once a month. They involve some lectures updating the staff on the latest research, best practice or changes needed in the hospital.

- e-portfolio – a relatively recent development of an online personal portfolio for each doctor to keep records of his or her training, log books of procedures, personal development plans and assessments on the job. This facility has centralized the training and assessment for junior doctors and specialist trainees, and also allows doctors to put in entries for reflections about their own practice. It is therefore a useful tool in shaping your educational needs, and maintaining an up-to-date e-portfolio is a requirement of an NHS doctor.

- Formal teaching – in the junior years (F1 and F2), there is a formal teaching programme that usually takes the form of lectures and training in the practical skills required of a junior doctor.

- Audit – a process by which the current practices in a hospital are compared to 'gold standards', such as national guidelines, to see how they might be improved. This process allows doctors to see shortcomings in their own practice, as well as to familiarize themselves with up-to-date policies on the investigation and treatment of patients.

- Courses – there are formal courses that doctors can attend which may be run by national societies in their particular branch of medicine. Surgical doctors may undergo specific training using equipment or procedures; for example, in laparoscopy (keyhole surgery using fibre-optic cameras) there are specific training courses that allow you to use the complicated devices involved.

Learning task

Try to attend a teaching session, departmental meeting or grand round on your work experience so that you can witness first-hand how both junior and senior doctors undertake on-the-job learning. This will also enable you to refer to and reflect on your experience in question 73 and similar questions. You could also ask to see each doctor's e-portfolio and ask the person what he or she gains from using it.

74. How will your A-levels help in your career in medicine?

This answer will vary from candidate to candidate depending on the subjects you are undertaking. Below are some of the points for consideration in your answers.

- Chemistry is a prerequisite for most medical courses, and is certainly worth mentioning. Ion and electrolyte chemistry forms the cornerstone of functional systems in terms of the cell and the role of the cell membrane. An in-depth knowledge of the various types of bonding will help a student appreciate how the drugs interact as well as how they might be designed.

- Biology. The study of anatomy and physiology in biology helps us to build up a picture of the human body in terms of structure and function. In particular, knowledge of the cell, and how it functions, allows us to understand when it goes wrong, and how we might go about correcting it. Knowledge of enzymes, structure and function, will help.

- Mathematics. There may be important calculations one needs to undertake involving medications, for example doses of drugs that must be given based on a patient's mass. Statistics are important in determining the significance of findings in research, as well as assessing the value of certain diagnostic tests.

- Physics. Volumetric relationships are important in the functioning of the body. For example, it can be helpful to understand Poiseuille's Law, which relates flow in a vessel to length, and the radius to the fourth power. Therefore we can understand that small changes in the radius of a vessel may greatly affect flow, and this is significant in the blood flow in vessels which may be narrowed by atherosclerosis.

75. Tell us about a scientific or medical development that has been in the news lately that you found interesting. Why has this interested you?

This question will require advance preparation to answer, not only in having read relevant articles, but also in thinking about how to formulate your answer. Consider the following points.

Try to do some reading related to the subject around the topic you have chosen. For example, if you are discussing a recent development in the treatment of rheumatoid arthritis, make sure you understand what the condition is (an autoimmune disease that causes inflammation in the joints), relevant tests that can help make the diagnosis (a certain antibody called rheumatoid factor is detected in a high percentage of patients) and what the treatments are (steroids, gold-based drugs and drugs that suppress the immune system). You can then link the new treatment in with your background knowledge to show a deeper understanding than simply having read one article out of the context of the disease.

It is difficult to predict what will be in the news in and around the time of your interview, so you should keep up to date with scientific current affairs. If you are doing significant scientific reading of journals such as the New Scientist, Student British

Medical Journal and others such as those listed on the next page, you should have a good grip on what the latest developments in the field are. If your story is taken from normal newspapers or their websites, they will probably contain a less in-depth analysis than the journal articles, which will require your outside reading to be more thorough if you are to give a fluent, interesting and informed answer.

Example answer

'I recently read an article proposing a mechanism of action for the pain-killing effect of acupuncture. My understanding is that there is some evidence base to suggest that acupuncture is effective for pain relief in certain conditions such as osteoarthritis, which is wear and tear of the joints. I believe there are some NICE guidelines that suggest GPs can refer a patient to acupuncture if first-line medications are not proving effective, and this suggests that there is both efficacy and value for money in this treatment for certain conditions. There have even been trials involving placebo needles with a control group that show a significant difference in pain control with acupuncture. However, the researchers who wrote the article had found that levels of adenosine, which is a neurotransmitter than can bind to receptors on the nerve cells and trigger an action potential, are raised in the area next to the needling. In particular, it is involved in the signalling of pain, and thus there may be a physiological explanation to a previously unexplained phenomenon.'

Learning task

Try to explain an interesting piece of medical news to friends, seeing how long you can maintain their interest. If you find they become disinterested quickly, try to change the way you approach the organization, expression and description, and find another 'victim' to practise on. This way, you can learn what does and doesn't work with both direct and indirect feedback from your friends. It is best if your test subjects do not know that they are being 'experimented' on, as they will give a more genuine response, and this allows you to build up an understanding of what techniques are valuable in storytelling, and which are not.

76. Do you read any medical publications, and if so, can you tell me about something interesting that you have read?

The answer to this question follows a similar pattern to the answer to question 75, but refers to more in-depth medical publications. Use a similar structure to **describe** the article and **link in** your own knowledge.

Recommended reading

- *Student British Medical Journal (sBMJ)*;

- *British Medical Journal (BMJ)*;

- *The Lancet*;

- *The New England Journal of Medicine (NEJM)*.

77. Do you read any scientific publications, and if so, can you tell me about something interesting that you have read?

This question carries a different emphasis from question 76, which was limited to medical journals. You can broaden your answer to include scientific as well as medical journals, such as those from the reading list below.

Recommended reading

- *New Scientist*;

- *Nature*;

- *Scientific American*.

78. What does being 'on call' mean?

A hospital must still maintain its function on evenings, weekends and overnight. This means that although most doctors will work a 9 am to 5 pm shift, there will be a rota for covering 'out-of-hours' work, which is known as the on-call system. This involves a skeleton team of doctors covering acute events and emergencies during this time. There will be a rota such that you will only be covering this duty every so often, with a number of on-call duties per month.

On-call shifts can be very busy, involving seeing patients you are unfamiliar with and treating them. It is also an excellent learning opportunity, where you are able to be more directly involved in decision making from a junior level. Doctors will typically be on call for a number of nights in a row, and then allowed a day or two to readjust their internal clock to daylight hours. Consultants also work on call, but can usually remain offsite and be contacted via phone for advice.

The relative disruption to your normal routine caused by on-call shifts continues all the way to the end of your specialist training years. This is a consideration that is often overlooked by many applicants, and understanding this system will help prepare you for the rigours of the career ahead.

79. What are the dangers of being a doctor?

These can be divided into physical dangers and legal dangers.

Physical dangers

Infectious diseases

Many medical procedures, such as injections, cannulation and operations, require use of sharp instruments on patients. An intravenous cannula is a plastic device used to gain entry into the venous system, and can remain in place for some time. It is then used to inject medications into the veins without having to pierce the vein repeatedly. As a junior doctor, you will have to place hundreds of IV cannulas. With each procedure, there are associated risks. The first of these is physical injury, if you stab yourself with the needle. However, more frightening is the so-called needle-stick injury, where you stab yourself with a needle contaminated with a patient's blood. There are several serious blood-borne diseases, such as HIV/AIDS and hepatitis C (a virus that attacks the liver), that can be contracted. Hepatitis C has a relatively increased frequency in intravenous drug-user patients, and cannot be cured. HIV/AIDS can be treated with anti-retroviral therapy but there is no definite cure. Medical students and doctors currently require hepatitis B vaccinations in order to practice to prevent them acquiring that disease. Overall, this means that even on the nights when you are most tired at work, you must ensure that you practise sharps safety or you can put yourself at serious risk.

Other airborne diseases such as tuberculosis (TB) or swine flu, are also a risk when in contact with patients. Measures such as wearing a mask are usually guided by hospital policy.

Occupational health problems

Occupational health problems may also arise. There are physical elements to a doctor's job, in some disciplines more than others, and doctors can suffer from chronic back pain or other physical health problems resulting from poor posture or repeatedly bending down to examine patients.

Assault

There is also a risk of assault. Doctors may be at risk of harm from patients who may be heavily intoxicated by alcohol or illegal drugs. Patients who are confused, due to an infection, electrolyte imbalance or psychiatric problem, can also be violent.

Legal dangers

● Poor medical practice can be punished by disciplinary measures up to and including being struck off the register by the General Medical Council (GMC).

- Poor practice resulting in the harm of a patient may be punishable under the tort law as negligence.

- Legal issues outside of the hospital such as illegal drug use or violence may be reported to the GMC and can also lead to dismissal.

80. How well do you cope with criticism?

Example answer

'I think that criticism can sometimes feel quite unpleasant, but at the same time I understand that it is useful and an important part of life, and I will try to treat it as such. However, as students in school we are exposed to criticism of our work, appearance and even performance in sports from peers, seniors and teachers. I suppose that even when criticism is useful, such as being told about a dishevelled appearance or poor choice of pass in football, the manner in which it is expressed affects the manner in which it is received. Therefore, what I would try to do is not focus on the harsh or painful elements of a criticism, if there are any, but to look instead at the key factual points that are being made. Usually criticism has a fundamental basis, and I would try to take this point on board, integrate it with what I know, and try to implement a change so that I would not make the same mistake again. If the error that has been made needs an apology, then I would also make sure to apologize appropriately.

If the criticism has no basis whatsoever, for example is factually inaccurate, then it may not appear to be useful. However, one can only make this assumption after a thorough investigation of what they are doing and so even if the criticism is inaccurate, it may prompt me to look at what I do in detail and think about it, and so it would have been useful for triggering that self-reflective process.'

Points to note

The key points are that this student:

- accepts that criticism can be difficult to take at times;
- recognizes the importance of criticism in personal development;
- disentangles the objective information from the emotional element;
- looks ahead to future practice.

These points form the basis of reflective practice.

81. How has information technology had an impact on the NHS?

The present

● Increased legibility. There is often a team of doctors involved in a patient's care, as well as other members of the health care team, and medical notes are vital to pass on the information about what conditions the patient has, what has been done for the patient so far and what is still outstanding. Issues can arise when poor handwriting in a doctor makes it hard to decipher this medical trail, but electronic notes have removed that problem.

● Increased speed. In some areas, information technology has increased the speed at which information is transferred. For example, when a patient has a blood test, the tubes are sent to the laboratory, processed and the results then made available on computer systems for the doctor to access. This is far faster than sending the results printed on paper and much more manageable than calling all the doctors for all of the results.

● Confidential data safety. Patients' notes contain potentially sensitive information and can be at risk of being accessed by third parties, particularly if password information is not regulated closely.

● Environmental impact. Theoretically, electronic notation and letters will allow the saving of the vast amounts of paper used in hospital and other settings at present, improving the carbon footprint of the NHS. However, this benefit will be offset in part by the increased use of electricity when referring to and inputting notes.

The future

● The possibility of doctor–patient consultations from a distance is becoming increasingly viable with advancing information technology. Simple possibilities include GP consultations via webcam – although there will always be the problem of not being able physically to examine the patient, there are some problems that may be more amenable to remote investigation than others. There may be more advances such as remote consultations on the ward using a computer with a camera and screen, on a trolley.

● The use of robotics in surgery can improve the accuracy of incisions by removing the human element of tremor.

● Surgical procedures can be further improved by technology in tactile feedback and three-dimensional viewing.

82. Can you tell us about any significant medical stories in the media at the moment?

This question is similar to question 75 ('Tell us about a scientific or medical development that has been in news lately that you found interesting. Why has this interested you?') and can be approached in a similar way. However, there are some significant differences, as it is not asking only for science and medicine-related developments, which suggests research findings. It can also include medical news such as:

● developments in the NHS, for example proposals to let GPs run their own budgets for prescribing in their practices;

● high-profile rogue doctor cases, for example those of Dr Shipman or Dr Ubani;

● medico-legal news, such as developments in rulings from the European Court of Human Rights that affect us;

● hospital scandals, for example the Mid Staffordshire Hospital report showing excess deaths due to poor practice, and patients drinking water from vases because they were so thirsty.

You can therefore use this question as an opportunity to focus more on the social, medico-legal or administrative sides of medicine if you feel that you have covered scientific material sufficiently in the interview so far, or vice versa. If you are unsure about what type of story to quote, bear in mind that traditional medical schools may be more interested in seeing your ability to engage in in-depth scientific discussion, whereas PBL schools may wish to see how you deal with the sociological impacts of medicine.

83. Can you tell us about something in the history of medicine that interests you?

Discoveries you may wish to refer to include:

● the discovery of penicillin;

● sterile technique in operations;

● the discovery of the DNA double helix by Watson and Crick;

● imaging and X-rays;

● stem cell research;

● smallpox and vaccination.

Try to read several articles about the same event to integrate several perspectives into your answer.

84. What do you think is the most important advancement in the medical field in the last 100 years?

This is a very common question that students report having been asked at their interviews. They fell into two groups when it was asked, either well prepared or completely stumped. Ensure that you are in the former group by picking one or two important advances and reading up on them.

Important advances you may wish to refer to include the following:

- Information technology – which has influenced the development in speed and security of information, allowing doctors to remotely access laboratory results or images, and therefore more quickly use this information to guide the treatment of a patient.

- 'Designer' pharmaceuticals – this advancement in the intelligent design of drugs, which has moved away from the more chance use of products in the environment, such as plants or fungi, uses knowledge of the molecular structure of certain targets to design drugs to enhance or inhibit them. You may wish to refer to specific drugs such as enfuvirtide, which is an anti-HIV drug. (You may find it helpful to ask a doctor how to pronounce this, or other tongue-twister drugs.)

- Imaging such as X-ray, CT and MRI – for example, X-rays have allowed us to take a two-dimensional picture of the body, which is useful for looking at issues such as fractures, lung infections or abdominal obstruction. However, CT scans (computed tomography scans) take a series of X-rays from different directions and use a complicated algorithm to synthesize a three-dimensional image, allowing us to see inside the body with great detail, which is especially useful for the planning of surgery and cancer treatment. MRI scans involve using changes in the magnetic resonance of hydrogen atoms to provide a three-dimensional image of the body without exposure to harmful X-rays.

- Genetic testing of babies – we now screen for serious genetic diseases in babies by sampling the DNA from cells either in the amniotic fluid sac or from the placenta, potentially preventing babies being born with diseases such as spina bifida or Down's syndrome. However, this technology also has the frightening capacity to cause ethical problems, such as sex-selection of babies, which is currently illegal in this country but may occur in non-regulated settings.

● Doctor–patient concordance rather than compliance. This would be an interesting choice of selection. You may wish to preface this choice with a qualifying statement such as 'Although I appreciate the value of technical advancements, such as MRI imaging, or designer pharmaceuticals, such as antiretroviral drugs targeting specific elements of HIV replication, I think the greatest change has been in the attitudes to the doctor–patient relationship...' in order to avoid seeming too unscientific.

85. What do you think of the fact that nurses are now undertaking tasks that were previously done by doctors?

Example answer

'I think that there are certain things nurses can do that doctors have previously done. For example, on my work experience I noticed that the junior doctors were often fitting intravenous cannulas, but when they had trouble in patients with difficult or small veins, they would often ask for help from senior nurses who had good experience with them.

From the economic point of view, for the NHS it is cheaper to run a nurse-led diabetic screening clinic, for example, than a doctor-led one. However, in nurse-led clinics, there should always be the provision to call a doctor for a second opinion if there is a patient with symptoms that may warrant further investigation or if the nurses feel they cannot manage alone.

I think, however, that there are some tasks that should be undertaken only by doctors, such as physical examination, diagnosis, investigation and formulation of a treatment plan. I am not exactly sure how much anatomy, physiology or pharmacology nurses study, but since the nursing degree takes three years and a medical degree lasts five years, by sheer mathematics there must be some significant differences. Therefore, I think it is a good thing for both members of the team when nurses undertake some tasks previously done by doctors, as long as the nurses have sufficient training if needed, and with the provision to refer to a doctor if necessary.'

86. What difficulties might be faced by a person with a major physical disability pursuing a career in medicine?

You can use this question to demonstrate your in-depth knowledge of the requirements of the job of a doctor.

These are some of the difficulties that may be faced:

● Emergency situations may require a doctor to move quickly, for example in the event of a cardiac arrest, where time is vitally important.

● Surgery requires considerable dexterity and coordination, and a person with some conditions such as motor neurone disease or early-onset Parkinson's disease may struggle.

- Social stigma may still exist for the doctor with a severe disability, and some patients may consider, for example, HIV infection as a negative characteristic, and not wished to be treated by a sufferer.

- Disabilities relating to communication may cause difficulties in doctor–patient interactions.

Points to note

Ensure that you do not sound prejudiced yourself by adding concrete reasons behind each of the disadvantages that you discuss. Soften the impression of your answers by using phrases such as 'may affect...' or 'could have an impact on the person's ability to...'.

There may also be some advantages, such as a doctor with a major physical disability having greater empathy for patients with a similar condition, as the doctor will have personal experience of it.

Summary

- Being able to answer the questions in this chapter is vitally important, as it demonstrates your consideration of a career as a doctor, in addition to your knowledge of the science aspect.

- This section also reflects the area in which you can most distinguish yourself from other candidates, as their knowledge in this area is typically theoretical or non-existent.

- Always strike a balanced opinion and discuss the pros and cons before coming to a conclusion.

- This material may be difficult to find elsewhere, but reflecting on your own experiences of talking to doctors can help.

- Understanding medicine as a profession as well as a subject is a sign of careful consideration and research into your career choice.

- Speaking to doctors and current medical students is a good way to prepare for this section.

- Try to present both sides of the argument before coming to a balanced conclusion on the more controversial topics.

CHAPTER 9

Hospital life and the NHS

Introduction

As an aspiring doctor, you are not only applying for a position at medical school, but in a sense you are applying for a job as well. All trainees spend two years in hospital after they graduate, and some significant time inside the hospital on attachments at medical school, so it is reasonable that admissions tutors might expect you to have some idea what you are letting yourself in for. It will help to be able to refer to work experience memories and encounters, as well as discussions with doctors and medical students (as mentioned previously, such as in Chapter 8) as these will be your main sources of information.

The NHS is the government body that will be your employer in the future, and therefore it is pragmatic to have an understanding of it, its core values, its various bodies and functions. Moreover, you should be concerned with the well-being of the health of the nation as a doctor, and the NHS is the means by which the vast majority of health care is delivered. As it is a government body, political agendas will often have an impact on it, for better or for worse, and it is a doctor's responsibility to be aware of news regarding the NHS that might affect the way that patients are treated.

This chapter gives details of some of the common questions candidates have encountered that are specifically concerned with hospital life and the NHS, and gives some factual information that may be helpful in broadening your knowledge on the subject.

Questions

87. How does the hospital function at night and what problems might be encountered?

You may wish to consider these points. The hospital at night will have fewer staff than during the daytime, and as such the on-call team (see question 78) will have to deal with the problems involving patients. There are usually even fewer doctors on call at night, so if things become busy their services can be stretched. However, there will still need to be a presence:

- at the accident and emergency department, and medical and surgical admissions unit, to assess patients needing to come into hospital;

- at surgical theatres, in case of the need for emergency operations that cannot wait, such as for ruptured appendix or ruptured abdominal aortic aneurysm (a rupture in a swelling of the main blood vessel in the abdomen);

- on the wards, in case of problems developing with current in-patients;

- by the cardiac arrest team, to attend and manage cardiac arrests when a patient's heart stops beating.

Other issues to consider are that support services may be closed or limited, so, for example, if you require a particular drug, it may need to be obtained from the emergency pharmacy or borrowed from another ward. There can be security issues with lower staffing levels, but there are always security staff available to come and assist with problems such as violent or agitated patients.

Learning task

If you can get permission, try to undertake a work shadowing of a junior doctor on a night shift. You may be able to see many different departments, attend medical emergencies and observe the doctor managing issues such as patients' pain or anxiety which may keep them awake. You may also find the doctor has more time to explain to you what he or she is doing and it will be a great learning experience to refer to in interview. You may wish to undertake this during your holidays, however, as I am sure you will be unable to attend school the next day.

88. How do doctors relax and socialize in the hospital setting?

Some students have been asked this or similar questions either as a follow-up to questions about stress management (see question 58), or as a follow-up to a question related to work experience. While doctors will be on duty in the hospital setting, it is important for them to have breaks.

Example answer

'I found the most enjoyable lunches were when the whole team would come for lunch in the canteen. It was interesting to see another side of each of the doctors and feel that senior and junior doctors alike could discuss current affairs, sports or medical news freely. In terms of relaxing, there was a doctor's mess that had a television, computers and a pool table – but most importantly it was a place where different doctors from different specialties could catch up with each other. There were also events such as an annual ball and payday dinners. I think this was nice to see as doctors will have to work as a team and such activities bring people together, which I think makes them want to work for each other and support one another when needed.'

89. What are the origins of the NHS?

The NHS was founded as a post-war entity in 1948 that was to provide free health care to the whole population of the UK, funded from the government. Prior to its inception, people had to pay for their medical services as and when they needed them, or take part in private health insurance paid from a proportion of their wages.

The main principles were that health care was to be free at the point of use, that everyone was eligible for it and that it should be funded by taxation. The basic structure of the NHS was that primary care (GPs) should see patients in the community and refer them on to secondary care specialists (who would be hospital based) if necessary. Other services such as vaccination and midwifery were also available in the community.

The NHS went on to be more expensive than it was originally envisaged, and this soon precipitated the use of prescription charges, then overall caps of the budget for the NHS and, later, the introduction of managers to assume responsibility for the finances of hospitals, who came into place under Margaret Thatcher's government in the 1980s. Understanding the origin and the aims of the NHS will be helpful in showing your understanding of how health care in this country is run today, and where this system originates from.

90. What does the NHS do?

As we have seen from the points following question 89, the key role of the NHS is to provide free health care at the point of use, funded from central taxation. Functions of the NHS include:

- provision of routine medical services, in the first instance by consultation with a GP;
- provision of medications, secondary to a prescription charge except to exempt groups, such as children and the elderly;
- provision of emergency medical care, including the ambulance service;
- public health education and disease prevention programmes;
- family planning and maternity services;
- vaccination programmes.

91. What roles do managerial staff play in the NHS?

These are some of the managerial roles.

The chief executive officer (CEO) will be in charge of the hospital from the overall business perspective. The CEO will determine the budgets for departments, employment policies, staffing levels and, together with medical staff, priorities for treatment.

Hospital rota managers coordinate the on-call shifts of the medical staff. This is a very busy job, particularly if doctors wish to switch their on-call duties with other staff members in order accommodate events such as annual leave.

Bed managers play an important role in organizing how patients coming into the hospital are allocated to appropriate wards for medical or surgical intervention. They will also liaise with staff responsible for infection control about how isolation or side-rooms are being used to minimize the spread of serious infections such as MRSA.

In some hospitals there is a managerial position in charge of **racial and sexual equality**. This manager plays an important role in support of ethic and religious minorities in the workforce and organizes events and training for staff.

Ward managers are senior nurses who fundamentally replace the 'matron' of previous generations. They play a key role in how the ward operates in terms of infection control, staffing issues, nursing care, training, equipment, patient monitoring and many other important functions.

Postgraduate centre staff are responsible for the training of doctors, particularly junior doctors, and help to provide advice for training courses, in-hospital teaching, examinations and careers advice.

92. What is wrong with the NHS?

The problems that you may wish to refer to include the following.

Administration

The NHS is often accused of having poor efficiency in terms of spending and organization. There are arguments that allowing free market economics of competition would increase the overall efficiency of hospitals and trusts (which are in charge of hospitals within certain areas). However, the consumers (patients) may not be free to move around and choose the hospital of their choice owing to their illness or the urgency of the problem requiring medical attention, and thus a simple free competition may not work.

Possible solutions

● Allow limited competition.

● Undergo assessment from independent consulting firms who can bring the expertise of organization from other industries and/or countries and apply them to the UK system.

● Allow doctors to play an important role in advising administration staff how to optimize the current system.

● Hire organization staff with excellent business backgrounds, including senior managers and MBA graduates, to improve efficiency.

Funding

Funding is always a limiting factor in medical treatment and at present the only source of funding is through government revenues, primarily tax. Tax is split to fund various services such as education, transport, the military and health. Changing the way the NHS is funded may be a difficult thing, but we will always have to strike a balance between improving public services and over-taxation.

Waiting lists

Waiting for operations, procedures and investigations can be distressing for patients. For those with certain conditions, such as some types of cancer, a delay in their treatment can allow further spread and cause more harm.

Possible solutions

At present there are 'fast-track' initiatives to ensure that patients with diseases that have time-sensitive diagnoses, such as some cancers, are seen by a specialist within two weeks. The 'choose and book' system allows patients to look at a timetable and pick out certain available slots for their appointment with specialists. This has somewhat streamlined the allocation system compared with the previous one when patients were simply given a fixed time slot. It means that since they are choosing, they are more likely to be available and therefore not miss their appointment, which would have increased waiting list times by wasting spaces in clinics or investigations.

Postcode lottery

This refers to the fact that each NHS Trust is able to set its own policy regarding the prescription of drugs or treatment, including based on cost-effectiveness. Therefore, if you have a disease that requires an expensive treatment, you may or may not receive that treatment, depending on where you live.

> Be careful not to be over-critical of the NHS, as although it may have its problems, it also provides a valuable public service. Also, doctors will inevitably have worked or be working for the NHS and may be proud of the service that it provides. Heavy criticism that is not justified with reasoning may not be well received by some members of your interview panel, and this could go against you, so just ensure that your answers are well balanced.

93. Who is the current minister of health?

> Question 93 is a simple one, but one particular student replied 'I don't know actually, but can I ask, why do I need to know this?' The interviewer responded 'Because in essence this man, who is Andrew Lansley by the way, is your boss, and if you are applying for a job, it makes sense to know who your boss is going to be.'
>
> In a medical career, while your 'boss' at work is more realistically the consultant in charge of your area, the head of the specialty department, the director of medicine or the CEO of the hospital, it is also true that the current minister of health is your boss. More importantly, if you know who it is this shows that you have a general awareness of medical news and current affairs. Politics plays an important role in medicine and the Department of Health is simply another government department, so having some awareness of such matters is relevant and demonstrates your interest.

94. Was sending men to the Moon a waste of money?

This question has come up on a number of occasions and students have reported that they are unsure of what it is driving at. There are two essential elements with regard to a medical school interview. The first relates to rationing of limited resources – could this money have been spent more beneficially on other things, in particular health services (but equally transport infrastructure or education)? The second is: how valuable is the pursuit of scientific knowledge?

Here are some points you may wish to consider:

- Sending men to the Moon was a technological feat that required considerable advances in engineering, computing and ballistics. The drive for this achievement stimulated progress in these fields and we enjoy many of the benefits today in air travel, iPods and GPS navigation.

- NASA and other space agencies stimulate the economy by providing contracts for the construction of spacecraft, as well as jobs in research and administration that are filtered back down to the general population by the trickle-down effect as the employees spend money and pay taxes. It also reduces unemployment in the countries concerned.

- Sending men to the Moon was a particular end point in the space race in the Cold War between the USSR and the USA and may in some part have contributed to the avoidance of a military conflict, in conjunction with other events.

- The pursuit of scientific knowledge to understand our Universe and our place in it is a valuable one, and some would say a fundamental need of our civilization.

- The money spent on space exploration and missions to the Moon could have been spent on other services such as health and education. This would not only have benefited that generation, but would also have gone on to have further positive effects on increasing overall literacy and numeracy rates in a population. It could also have reduced the disease burden within a population.

Summary

- This chapter details several key issues that you should know about in detail, in order to give a considered and informed impression to the interview panel.

- One of the key sources of knowledge for you in answering these questions is your own work experiences and reading up on the NHS.

- Talking to doctors and other multidisciplinary team members about current affairs will aid your knowledge base.

- Supplement this with the theoretical information contained within this chapter to give balanced answers.

CHAPTER 10

Medical knowledge

Sources of knowledge

Preparation tips

Many medical school interviewers are moving away from testing the body of medical knowledge of candidates. This is because they feel that students will be able to learn these concepts at medical school, and they are more interested in testing potential. Therefore, the number of questions related to medical diseases and conditions they ask is less than it was 10 or 15 years ago.

However, general medical knowledge questions do occur in several contexts in interviews nowadays. First, if you have claimed to have an interest in science, asking you to talk through the biology of a disease is a good way to see how you apply the principles of biology and chemistry to a scenario. Interviewers may test how you explain your knowledge, which may reflect how you may communicate information about a disease to patients in the future.

Oxbridge interviews may take this principle further, and explore all the scientific elements of a disease from genetics, risk factors, physiology, investigation and treatments. You may end up discussing a disease you have never heard of before, and the examiners will give you clues to help you draw upon your own knowledge to answer the question. The method for answering this type of problem is given in Chapter 14.

Other types of medical knowledge questions that occur with increasing frequency in interviews are related to the NHS, other governmental and non-governmental bodies and how the practice of medicine is regulated. Admissions tutors have stated that one method for testing a candidate's rounded knowledge of the medical profession is by challenging the person to interpret and explain current affairs in the medical world. This chapter provides example questions and hints to help you develop the skills to navigate these challenges as well as form a solid basis of knowledge.

Questions

General

95. What is health?

It will be helpful to know the World Health Organization's definition of health, which encapsulates the spirit of a holistic approach to health: 'Health is a state of complete physical, mental and social well-being and not merely the absence of disease or infirmity.' This definition is important when we consider that we as doctors may be focused on treating the physical health of patients, but other aspects such as their social well-being in particular are often neglected, despite having a large impact on their quality of life. Psychiatrists deal with the mental health of patients if those patients suffer from a formal disorder. However, social well-being is more complex and encompasses ideas such as family life, support networks including friends, home environment and self-esteem. In short, curing a patient of diseases is not the enough for the promotion of health. In order to do that, we must consider various aspects of a patient's life and may need to involve other members of the multidisciplinary team such as physiotherapists, occupational therapists and social workers.

96. What is the Hippocratic Oath and what does it mean to doctors nowadays?

Example answer

'The Hippocratic Oath dates back to ancient Greece, where Hippocrates was a scholar and physician, and is an oath taken by doctors both in the past, and, in a modified manner, in modern day. It is usually summarized as "First do no harm" which is a statement still valid today; indeed doctors can aspire to hold this true, although there are some treatments with known significant side-effects or risk of harm. There are some outdated elements such as swearing to the God Apollo, the patron of knowledge and the healing arts, which are no longer relevant today. There are also references which prohibit the giving of drugs that may cause a patient to die, effectively euthanasia, which is still illegal today. However, the oath also includes

*a clause excluding doctors from performing abortions, which does not fit into modern
medicine, at least legally.*

*Another clause states you should refrain from engaging in sexual relations with either slaves or
freemen that you treat and is still very valid today in preventing abuses of the doctor–patient
relationship that would damage the reputation of the profession. In many medical schools this
has now been made with a declaration.'*

97. How do politics influence health care provision and is this inevitable?

Consider the following issues. Politicians decide the distribution of wealth to various
services – education, military, transport and health. Therefore, politics are important
in setting the health care budget and determine the amount of money we have available
to spend on the investigation and treatment of our patients. Politics are also
involved in funding for scientific research and can influence the development of
new treatments for existing diseases, which has a very real impact on the population
at large.

There may be some political influence on the way we practice. For example, high-
profile medical cases such as Dr Ubani, a locum GP from Germany involved in the
overdose and death of a patient with morphine, may cause changes in the way
medical practice is regulated.

Legislation is a political process, and the legal position for certain policies such as
abortion, organ donation and stem cell research are set by politicians. They may be
advised by independent bodies of scientists in order to come to their decision.

Cases such as the MMR link to autism may become a popularized or sensational-
ized story, which causes public health issues for the whole population, in this case by
reducing the uptake of vaccinations, making children vulnerable to serious disease. The
government may also take an active role in epidemics of disease, issuing vaccinations
to vulnerable groups such as in the swine flu outbreak, or even quarantining patients
who were suspected of having SARS, as occurred in certain regions of China during
the outbreak.

98. Do you think doctors should set a good example to their patients in their own lives? How or why might this be difficult?

This question requires you to consider whether or not, as professionals in a position
of trust, doctors are expected to act with integrity in their personal lives as this reflects
how they may act professionally. You may wish to discuss whether or not this is a fair
comparison, and the fact that doctors are humans too, and may make mistakes
professionally or personally.

99. In what ways do you think doctors can promote good health, other than through direct treatment of illness?

Example answer

'Doctors can promote good health on the individual scale by discussing with patients their lifestyles, in the clinic or hospital setting. This can be an important method for having direct impact on a patient's life. Doctors are able to provide information and recommendations for support organizations, and can even provide some pharmacological support, such as nicotine patches or inhalers to aid efforts to stop smoking. I understand that as part of the clinical communication skills training, we will learn about how to implement these health behaviour changes, and that these interactions are more focused on negotiation than telling patients what they should and shouldn't do.

On the larger scale, doctors can become involved in public health initiatives such as government campaigns, which can involve media such as newspapers, radio and television, to promote healthy behaviours.'

This answer includes several key elements for success; first, it organizes the answer into small and large scale so it is easier for the interviewers to follow. It also demonstrates knowledge of the course and, in particular, communication skills, which may be most helpful for PBL and integrated courses.

Other examples to consider include:

- leading a healthy and balanced lifestyle as a doctor as an example to the population the doctor is treating;

- attention to the mental health of the population, by raising awareness of conditions and reducing the stigma associated with mental health disorders by promoting understanding of the conditions as diseases rather than blaming the individual sufferers;

- individual efforts (in the role of the person rather than as a doctor) including health-oriented activities such as 'Race for Life' running, or raising money and awareness for certain conditions.

100. What is NICE?

NICE is the National Institute for Health and Clinical Excellence. It is an NHS-based organization with the purpose of making recommendations to the NHS regarding treatments, cost effectiveness and evidence base. It issues information in the form of guidelines that doctors can use in assessing which treatments to prescribe under certain conditions. For example, in the treatment of rheumatoid arthritis, it recommends the use of cheaper agents such as steroids or methotrexate, as opposed to expensive monoclonal antibody drugs. This is because many people will show improvement after using the cheaper drugs, and therefore it is cost-effective to save the expensive treatments for those who have tried the first-line drugs and had no effective response.

'NICE is a pattern of goodwill behaviour which elicits presents from Santa. Its antithesis is naughty.'

This was an amusing answer given by a student at an interview, but he admitted it was only because he had no idea what NICE stood for. Although this is certainly not a recommended approach, it was well received by the interview panel. It is far safer, however, to admit your lack of knowledge in a conventional manner and ask what an unknown term is; for example, 'I'm afraid I don't know.'

101. What is the BMA?

The British Medical Association is the union for doctors – an organization that represents the opinions of doctors to the public, the government and the press. It is a voice for the medical profession as a body. It provides support, careers advice and teaching courses for doctors.

It also publishes a bimonthly journal, the *British Medical Journal* (*BMJ*); and the *Student British Medical Journal* (*sBMJ*), which many students read as an entry-level journal in preparation for pre-interview reading. These journals contain research mostly undertaken and written by doctors.

102. What is the GMC?

The GMC stands for the General Medical Council, and it is the professional regulatory body for doctors. It deals with disciplinary issues and doctors' registration as well as providing guidance about good practice of medicine. Patients can also use it to check the registration of their doctor to see that the person is genuinely qualified and not under investigation for any misconduct issues.

Many students understandably confuse the roles of the BMA and the GMC. The key difference is that the BMA represents doctors, whereas the GMC regulates doctors.

It may be useful to read the sections of the GMC publication *Duties of a Doctor* that give details of professional behaviours and standards. You could then refer to some of these in your answer to question 102, as well as other questions, particularly regarding law and ethics. See www.gmc-uk.org for more details.

103. What is meant by evidence-based medicine?

Evidence-based medicine is a practice of using treatments and interventions that have evidence or data to support their use. In practice, this means that the treatments have undergone clinical trials, comparing them against placebos or alternative drugs, and have been shown to have a significant benefit.

Although it sounds as if doctors would have to read through all the research published on a particular treatment in order to practise evidence-based medicine, in reality hospitals publish guidelines that are carefully researched, so that all doctors can follow them. For example, the cardiology department might publish guidelines on which medications to prescribe after a heart attack, and all the doctors in the hospital can refer to these guidelines when dealing with patients in this situation.

104. What are the arguments for and against non-essential surgery being available on the NHS?

Non-essential surgery by its definition is surgery that is not necessary for the survival or improvement of a disease of a patient, and can include cosmetic surgery. In answering this question, use well-fleshed-out examples to demonstrate your knowledge that health is more than simply the absence of disease, and that patients may suffer, for example, psychological harm from having cosmetic issues that may be helped by surgery. On the opposite side, in a system of limited resources, treating physical harm may be preferred to treating psychological harm. Again, it can be helpful to refer to the World Health Organization's definition of health.

105. What does the current government see as the national priorities in health care and do you agree with these?

The Department of Health, under the auspices of the government, will be your future employer, and as such it is reasonable that their concerns will later become your concerns. It is important to keep up to date with the current situation, which you may glean by following the news as well as checking websites such as those for the Department of Health. This question's subject will change frequently, but the principles of answering remain the same, as it is important to address the mortality (rate of deaths) and morbidity (effect of the disease on a person's life), and seeing how many of the population are effected, and how severely. You may also wish to consider how easily a condition may be treated, and whether or not there are worsening conditions, eg childhood obesity in the UK may give rise to increasing rates of diabetes later.

106. Would you focus on preventing people from getting diseases or treating them when they are ill, and why?

Prevention of disease: it is often cheaper to prevent disease than treat it, as well as reducing the burden on the patient. Our understanding of disease processes and new drugs helps us in this aim, eg statins that reduce cholesterol, reducing the chances of heart attacks and strokes.

Treatment of disease: ill patients require treatment to reduce the impact on their lives, and this is one of the responsibilities of the profession. Not all diseases can be prevented, eg certain subtypes of lung cancer that occur in non-smokers, or genetic diseases.

107. Should doctors have a role in regulating contact sports, such as boxing?

Here are some points for the argument that doctors should have a regulatory role:

- Contact sports involve the risk of physical injury of a traumatic nature, and thus the opinions of doctors may be required in the treatment of participants in case of injury.

- Doctors may also be able to provide guidance on the safety measures undertaken by the sports – for example recommending head protection and gloves as worn in Olympic boxing events.

- The ethical principle of autonomy suggests that we should allow people to take part in contact sports. Furthermore, participants in sport are usually consenting, and so have the choice of whether or not to put themselves at risk.

Here are two points against this idea. Involvement in regulation would suggest that the medical profession supports or condones the activities. The ethical principle of non-maleficence states that doctors may not wish to encourage activities that are known to be harmful to others.

108. Do you think doctors should ever strike?

Strike action is voluntary and deliberate abstention from work and is one of the methods by which employment disputes are solved. It is a form of industrial action that is usually a last resort following negotiations. Most people will have experienced the effects of strikes involving transport staff that cause widespread disruption.

Although strike action is not taken lightly in other industries, in the medical profession it needs particularly serious consideration. Doctors are involved in the care of patients and have a critical responsibility to them. In the case of a strike by doctors, the only possible justification would be if the harm to the patients was outweighed by the value to the patients of the strike action. Realistically, this situation is unlikely to arise.

109. How does the NHS deal with the provision of very expensive treatments for individuals, in a system of limited resources?

There are several mechanisms by which the NHS rations its expenses, the first of which is guidance from NICE that integrates clinical effectiveness with value for money, as described in a previous question. Other tools include QALY, which stands for a 'quality-adjusted life year', and is a measurement that can be used to see how much patients would gain from a treatment. For certain expensive drugs such as Infliximab (a monoclonal antibody therapy for autoimmune disease), often there is a panel which will decide the outcome of a decision for a patient once proposed by a specialist, and this can involve a considerable amount of paperwork and bureaucracy.

110. Are different social and economic groups more vulnerable to certain diseases, and if so, why and what can be done about it?

The burden of diseases on different populations often varies, and in general lower socio-economic groups suffer from higher incidences of certain diseases, such as cardiovascular disease. Other diseases see a standard distribution across the various social groups, eg genetic disease.

Factors contributing to this distribution include:

● higher incidences of risk factors from lifestyle choices, eg smoking, high cholesterol diets;

● lower education.

What can be done about it?

● reduce the rich–poor divide within countries by taxation and wealth redistribution;

● increase lifestyle advice;

● increase accessibility to health care services for lower socio-economic groups.

111. What are the arguments for and against people paying for their own health care as and when they need it?

The main considerations we should take into account when contemplating a system of paying for one's own health care are clinical, moral and economic.

Example answer

'We can divide the arguments for and against people paying for their own health care into three categories: clinical, moral and economic. Starting with clinical, the main disadvantage of people paying for their own health care is that it might reduce the number of patients wishing to seek treatment as some would be put off by the cost. This would be worse for the patient clinically as delay in treatment might allow the disease to progress beyond our ability to treat it, for example with delay in receiving antibiotics for severe pneumonia, or having surgery for certain types of cancer. The advantage for people paying for their own health care is that it would reduce the amount of "worried well".

Morally, if we adopted this system we might be unfairly disadvantaging people who are less well off than others, as they could not afford to pay for treatments. In the long term, this might reduce the general health of this poorer demographic, which could in turn reduce their ability to find employment, which might compound the problem further. Economically, competition can lead to greater efficiency and thus the population as a whole may benefit. As it stands, the relative downsides of unfairly disadvantaging certain groups, in my mind, outweigh the costs of malingering patients and a less-efficient health care system, so I agree with the NHS provision of free health for all, at this time.'

A stratified and structured answer allows the interview panel to follow the dialogue more easily. Present the arguments for both sides before concluding with your own, balanced opinion.

112. Where does most medical treatment take place, inside or outside of hospital, and why?

Most medical treatment takes place in the community by GPs, such as consultations or prescriptions. Some of the reasons for this include:

- cost – keeping patients in hospital beds is expensive;
- comfort – patients often prefer to be treated in the home environment where possible;
- volume – hospitals simply cannot accommodate all patients who require treatment;
- organization – hospital care is generally reserved for emergency treatment, or specialist treatment.

113. What do you think about the way doctors are shown in the media and how do you think this will affect patients' views of their own doctors?

It can be helpful to divide this answer into factual versus fictional representation. In factual reporting such as documentary or news, there may be a tendency to report sensational news, eg rogue doctors or new research findings. In fiction, doctors may be portrayed as anything from saviours to villains. Dramatization of the medical environment can be both informative and misleading, and this may impact what your patients expect from you as a doctor in terms of treatment or behaviour.

114. What is the biggest health-related problem in the UK?

This question can have several potential answers, for example as follows:

● Obesity is an increasing problem in the UK, particularly with regard to childhood obesity, and this may involve secondary disease burdens such as osteoarthritis of the hips and knees, increasing heart disease and diabetes.

● Alcoholism is a significant problem. The binge-drinking culture in the UK can cause serious harm from violence or accidents during intoxication. Long-term alcohol abuse can be linked with liver cirrhosis and liver failure, as well as an increased risk of liver cancer.

● Smoking is linked strongly with heart disease, lung cancer and emphysema. However, with the effects of the recent smoking ban in public places, smoking rates are reducing and this answer might therefore be less of a priority than, for example, citing obesity, which is on the increase.

● Heart disease is the biggest killer in the UK. Smoking, obesity, diabetes, a high-cholesterol diet and lack of exercise can increase someone's chances of getting heart disease.

● Cancer is the second biggest killer in the UK, and is also important for the fear it causes in the population. One of the main features is that some types of cancer are hard to prevent or cure. However, it is also an important field as there are many breakthroughs in treatment and prevention, for example most recently the HPV vaccine for the prevention of cervical cancer.

115. Why do doctors no longer wear white coats?

Example answer

'I believe there are both physical and psychological reasons for this change in practice. On the physical side, white coats have long sleeves that may spread infection from one patient to another, especially when the doctor is physically examining patients. White coats may be

cleaned or changed less often than regular clothes, and therefore present a risk of harbouring infectious pathogens. Even ties are no longer allowed to be worn in hospital, again because of the risk of cross-infection.

On the psychological side, I believe that there is a move away from paternalism in the medical community, towards more patient-centric decision making. There is even a term 'white coat hypertension', where a patient's blood pressure can seem to be higher in a clinic than it is at home, due to the fear or anxiety surrounding the visit to the doctor. Of course, this is not due to the white coat itself, but what it represents. I believe that part of taking away the paternalistic pedestal of doctors is removing the symbols, of which the white coat is a very important one.'

116. Do you think more doctors or more nurses would be of greater benefit to the nation's health?

Doctors and nurses both form an important part of the health care team. You may wish to consider the following points:

- In the ward setting, more nurses would mean enhanced day-to-day care, allowing patients to be seen more frequently, and things such as changing, cleaning, drug administration and monitoring of baseline observations of pulse, blood pressure and respiratory rate could be undertaken more often.

- More nurses might also include the employment of specialist nurses who may deal with things such as acute pain management, diabetes screening or preoperative assessment – roles that have been previously held by doctors – and thus the increase in nurses would also lighten the workload for doctors, allowing them to perform more activities pertaining to diagnosis, investigation and management of patients.

- More doctors would be mean more availability for clinics, which would reduce waiting list times and result in conditions being treated faster. There would also be more presence on the wards to attend to problems with patients' health and larger surgical teams to undertake more operations per day, again reducing waiting times.

- In economic terms, employing more doctors would cost more than employing more nurses.

Important medical conditions

This section deals with commonly asked questions related to medical conditions and diseases. These can occur in the part of the interview dealing with your academic ability or also as a follow-up to other questions. For example, if you talked about a placement for work experience, it would be quite poor not to have gained from it a basic understanding of a heart attack, what it might be like and what treatments are available. Also, you should have a basic understanding of medically important diseases from your study of biology, and it would be poor not to be able to use this knowledge to discuss these conditions at interview.

117. What is HIV and AIDS; how is it transmitted and how can this be reduced?

HIV stands for human immunodeficiency virus, and does exactly what it says on the tin; it is a virus that causes a deficiency in the immune system of humans. However, the virus takes quite some time to manifest this deficiency, which it does by killing off a certain type of white blood cell in the body known as the CD4+ cell. This is because the CD4+ cell has a particular protein on its surface that allows the virus to bind to it and enter the cell. A low CD4+ cell count makes you vulnerable to infections, as CD4+cells are needed to fight off other bacteria and viruses. This is know as acquired immunodeficiency syndrome: AIDS. There are a number of 'AIDS-defining' conditions. For example, lung infections are common and AIDS makes you vulnerable to a particular bacteria type known as pneumocystis. Thus, you can have an HIV infection long before AIDS develops in you.

Genetics

It is a retro-virus, which carries its genetic code as RNA rather than DNA. Therefore, in order to integrate its code into your own cells and 'hijack' the protein production system, it must convert this RNA into DNA using an enzyme known as reverse transcriptase. Remember that transcription is the production of RNA from DNA, which occurs in your own cells as part of the protein manufacturing process.

Transmission

HIV is transmitted through bodily fluids, in particular blood, vaginal secretions and semen. Saliva is not infectious unless in very high quantities. Therefore unprotected sexual intercourse is one method by which HIV can be transmitted. Blood-borne transmission can occur in sharing contaminated needles, for example in injecting intravenous drugs such as heroin. For doctors there can be risk of contracting HIV if they accidentally stab themselves with a needle that they have been using on a patient (a 'contaminated needlestick' injury).

Prevention

One of the most important measures is using a barrier contraceptive such as a condom during sexual intercourse. Sex workers have a higher incidence of HIV infection, and risk activities such as unprotected sex with sex workers should be avoided. Education plays a key role in this element of prevention. Reduction of intravenous drug abuse, or clean needle exchange programmes, can help reduce the spread of HIV via the blood-borne route. More wide-ranging answers might include political stability, as several wars have seen rape used as a weapon of terror in genocide, which led to large increases of HIV.

118. What is swine flu?

Swine flu is an infection of a human by a virus that is normally found in pigs and which, due to mutations in its genetic code, became able to infect humans, and pass from human to human in droplets, for example through airborne spread by sneezing. Symptoms include chills, coughing, sneezing, fever, muscle pains, headache and sore throat. The global pandemic (see question 119 for a definition) of 2009 started in Mexico and spread rapidly around the around the world, causing over 15,000 deaths worldwide, with over 450 in the UK alone. This caused considerable concern among the public, which triggered policies for administering a vaccine to those who might be exposed, such as those in the health care industries and vulnerable groups such as children and the elderly.

119. What is a pandemic?

An epidemic is when a disease spreads rapidly and extensively, affecting many people in a population at the same time, to a degree that is more than would be expected normally. A pandemic is a global epidemic, which is to say a disease that spreads rapidly, affecting many countries in the world.

Famous pandemics in the recent past include SARS (severe acute respiratory distress syndrome virus) and swine flu, both of which caused thousands of deaths worldwide. The World Health Organization is the key international body that helps to coordinate the responses to pandemics and limits their effect by issuing policies and advice regarding treatment and isolation.

120. What are the leading causes of death in the UK?

- Heart disease is the leading cause of death in the UK, with acute myocardial infarction and heart failure included under this umbrella.

- One in four of all deaths in the UK are caused by cancer. Lung and colorectal cancers are the biggest killers, followed by breast cancer in women and prostate cancer in men.

- In young people, suicide, violence or accidental death are leading causes of mortality.

Many students report that question 120 is commonly followed up by 'What can you tell me about these diseases?', so be prepared to engage in a scientific discussion regarding the conditions you have described.

121. Do you think Jamie Oliver has affected the health of the nation?

This question is about the famous chef Jamie Oliver who ran a campaign to improve the food in schools, particularly from the nutritional point of view. The campaign was high profile in the media and helped to publicize the poor nutritional values of school food, particularly its saturated fats, high calories, high salt and low fruit and vegetable counts.

Example answer

'Raising awareness may be an important step in reducing childhood obesity, in the same way that cigarette packets now have pictures of mouth cancer and warning signs, which raises awareness of the risks. Obesity comes from too-high calorie intake coupled with a lower energy expenditure, and this campaign sought to tackle the intake element of the problem. Also, schoolchildren are not in control of the options, so that having only healthier options at school forces them to eat healthily. This may go on to have a knock-on effect on their choice of food outside of school, although this is not certain.'

Question 121 is also included to make an important point about dealing with unknowns; for those of you who are unfamiliar with Jamie Oliver or his campaign, this is the perfect opportunity to give a stupid or speculative answer if you are not careful. If you do not know particular places, people or events, you are unlikely to be able to reason out an answer, so be careful not to make wild guesses. Instead, simply state (in this case) 'I'm sorry, I don't know who Jamie Oliver is. Would you mind explaining who he is please?'

122. How would you try to combat childhood obesity?

Example answer

'Obesity is caused when there is an imbalance between energy input and energy output. Therefore the general approaches to combating obesity would be to promote exercise and activity, while at the same time increasing awareness of what constitutes a healthy diet. I might start on the energy output side by introducing compulsory exercise at school as well as introducing topics such as healthy eating to the school curriculum. Parents play a key role in selecting children's food. I might also undertake a publicity campaign for healthier foods, and ban crisps and chocolates from lunchboxes.

You could consider:

- banning the use of child-oriented mascots to advertise unhealthy foods;
- banning the advertising of unhealthy foods during peak hours of children's television;
- issuing guidelines to parents about a healthy lifestyle, including advice on activities and diet;
- government subsidies of healthy foods such as fruit and vegetables.

More adventurous examples include:

- implementing National Military Service that requires adolescents to undertake compulsory military training with a fitness component;
- promoting the use of 'active' video games such as Wii sports or Dance Revolution;
- financial incentives such as cheaper health insurance for those who have an optimal body mass index.

123. What do you know about asthma?

Asthma is a breathing problem that can be triggered by different factors, such as cold, exercise, pollen, dust or smoke. This type of asthma is known as extrinsic asthma. In contrast, intrinsic asthma has no known triggers and occurs for an unknown reason. Severe episodes of asthma can require hospital treatment, including artificial ventilation.

The main problem in asthma is that the airways leading to the lungs become swollen and narrow, which causes a decrease in the rate of air flow. This in turn reduces the amount of oxygen that can be taken in, and can lead to respiratory failure and death.

Treatment is usually by inhalers, which contain a steroid or other drugs that help to relax the airways and keep them open. Avoiding exposure to the triggers can also help prevent attacks.

124. Explain what a stroke is. Would you be able to recognize what was happening if someone you knew had a stroke?

The signs of a stroke include:

- slurred speech;
- weakness of one or multiple limbs;
- facial drooping.

The abbreviation 'FAST' has been used in a popular television commercial to make people aware of the symptoms of a stroke. This stands for 'Face, Arm, Speech, Time to call 999'. You may find it helpful as a pneumonic, as well as an interesting point to bring up in answering the question.

A stroke is the interruption of the blood supply to the brain. The brain requires a constant supply of oxygen to function, which it obtains via the bloodstream. There are many arteries and smaller vessels that supply specific areas, and when this is interrupted the cells in that area become damaged and die, which gives rise to the symptoms.

125. How would you know if someone you knew was having a heart attack and what would you do?

A heart attack occurs when the blood vessels supplying the heart become blocked and therefore there is insufficient oxygen supply to support the work of the heart.

HEART ATTACKS

The symptoms of a heart attack include:

- a crushing chest pain;

- shortness of breath;

- pain shooting down the left arm or up into the jaw;

- nausea and vomiting.

As for what you should do in the event of someone having a heart attack – call an ambulance as soon as possible. This is vital as the time at which a heart attack is treated is vitally important to its success; treatment with angioplasty (sending a balloon up the coronary arteries to dilate the blood vessels and clear a blockage), or dissolving of the clot blocking the artery (thrombolysis), can preserve heart muscle and improve survival rates.

Relax the patient into a comfortable position as activity or anxiety can increase the workload of the heart and therefore its demand for oxygen.

If the person stops breathing and you have had first aid training, you can perform CPR (cardiopulmonary resuscitation), which involves mouth-to-mouth inflations of the chest and chest compressions to pump blood around the body if the heart is not functioning.

126. Should children 'play in the dirt' more?

There are some theories stating that the reason more children are having allergies is that they are kept in increasingly sterile conditions and so their immune systems have fewer pathogens to fight against. The immune systems become hypersensitive because of this and 'fight' other, non-dangerous substances, such as peanuts, feathers or even the body itself (as in auto-immune diseases). Therefore, allowing your children to play in the dirt more may prevent this phenomenon.

> The evidence behind these theories is not concrete, and therefore you may wish to refer to them with a degree of academic caution, by stating only that this may be the case. In reference to question 122, it may be that increasing children's playing outdoors would also increase their energy output, and in conjunction with a healthy diet, this could reduce the problem of childhood obesity.

127. What is MRSA?

MRSA stands for methicillin-resistant *Staphylococcus aureus*. *Staphylococcus aureus* (SA) is a type of bacteria that lives on people's skin, and it is perfectly normal to have present. However, it can present problems when it gets past the barrier of the skin, such as into wounds or organs. We can usually treat these infections with antibiotics, but some strains of the bacteria can become resistant to the antibiotics by breaking them down with enzymes or pumping them out of their cells with special proteins in their cell walls. This means that the antibiotic treatment will be ineffective, and the patient's infection may become increasingly serious, which can result in death.

Methicillin is a type of penicillin, and therefore methicillin-resistant SA will be penicillin resistant, removing the first-line option for treatment. There are a few antibiotics that can still treat MRSA, such as vancomycin, but this is associated with some severe side-effects, and there are also now strains of vancomycin-resistant MRSA appearing. The relationship between bacteria and antibiotics can be viewed as a kind of 'arms race' in which new antibiotics are being developed in order to combat increasing resistance in bacteria. Finishing antibiotic courses, and reducing over-prescription of antibiotics, is important to reduce levels of resistance.

> The 'M' in MRSA does not stand for 'multi' as in 'multi-resistance SA', as many people seem to think.

128. What is *C. difficile?*

Clostridium difficile is a bacterial infection that causes severe diarrhoea in patients, and can be acquired in the hospital by patient-to-patient transmission, for example when a doctor examines one patient who is infected, and spreads the spores to the next patient. *C. difficile* is particularly difficult to deal with as the spores that it forms are physically tough and are not killed by the alcohol gels provided in hospital to cleanse hands. The spores are removed only by a thorough wash with anti-bacterial soap and water.

C. difficile is associated with a significant mortality, as patients lose a large amount of water and electrolytes from the diarrhoea and this dehydration can cause kidney failure or even death. Therefore, patients with *C. difficile* are isolated as soon as possible and wards having *C. difficile* outbreaks are cleared and undergo a deep cleansing to remove spores. *C. difficile* and MRSA are the two problematic hospital-acquired infections in the UK at present and it will be useful to be aware of these conditions.

Learning task

Ask the doctors and nurses on the wards about hospital-acquired infections and why they are so significant to their daily practice.

129. How are hospital-acquired infections prevented?

Example answer

'Hospital-acquired infections are prevented by sterile techniques, isolation and infection control policies. One of the main sources of infection in a hospital could be surgery, as the protective barrier of the skin is breached. Therefore, precautions must be taken during the operation. This includes the surgical team wearing "scrubs", which are clothes designed for wearing only inside the operating theatre. They must also "scrub up", which involves washing their hands with certain anti-bacterial soaps and using scrubbing pads to remove the bacteria normally present on the skin. I had a chance to do this in my work experience placement on a colorectal surgical team and I was made to do it very thoroughly indeed! Those on the surgical team also use sterile gloves, which are cleaned and then sealed, and must be put on in a certain manner to avoid touching the outside. A sterile gown is put on in a similar way, and again must not be touched by other things.

On the ward, patients are screened for MRSA by a laboratory test. In a hospital I visited, this was done by collecting swabs from their nose, armpits and groin. If they were MRSA positive, they would be put into a "side" room or isolation room and doctors and nurses treating them would have to wear a glove and gown to reduce the chances of transferring infection to other patients. Patients with unexplained diarrhoea are also isolated as this can be due to infectious bacteria such as C. difficile, which can cause fatal diarrhoea by loss of water.

There are several other infection control policies, such as not wearing white coats or ties because they may transmit infections. You may also be required to wash your hands, or use a self-evaporating alcohol gel when moving between bays or wards of a hospital.'

Points to note

The main methods of prevention can be categorized under two main headings: anti-bacterial products and prevention of spread.

130. What is diabetes?

Diabetes is a disease that is characterized by poor control of blood sugar. The hormone insulin is secreted from the pancreas and causes glucose to be taken up into cells and used or stored as glycogen. Diabetes occurs when either there is insufficient insulin produced (type I) or when the body becomes resistant to insulin and therefore glucose is not sufficiently removed from the bloodstream, leaving high levels in the blood (type II).

High sugar levels can cause secondary problems such as damage to the blood supply of certain organs or structures. Damage to the blood vessels supplying the nerves can cause a lack of feeling in the feet or loss of vision in the eye, and damage to the blood supply of the kidney can cause renal problems.

Treatment for type I diabetes involves the injection of insulin on a regular basis – this can be up to four times per day. This can be a difficult lifestyle, and the limitations in diet as well as constant monitoring of blood sugars and regular injections can be quite frustrating. There are new inventions that may decrease the need for such daily processes. The so called 'artificial pancreas' constantly monitors blood glucose levels and automatically adjusts the level of insulin administration through a needle under the skin.

131. What signs might indicate to you that your friend might be suffering from depression and what would you do about it?

The main feature of depression is a low mood, which may be observed (objective) as well as reported by the sufferer (subjective). You may notice that the person becomes more withdrawn and isolated, has less energy and has emotional fluctuations, such as becoming tearful.

Physical signs of depression include:

- poor appetite;
- low energy levels;
- disturbed sleep;
- poor concentration.

You could talk to your friend, and see if you could help him or her in some way. Simply discussing the issues might help your friend resolve them. If you were significantly worried, you could consult your friend's parents or a teacher who might be able to intervene further. You friend may need medical help with antidepressant therapy.

132. What is cancer?

Cancer is an uncontrolled growth of cells in the body. It occurs due to mutations in the DNA code of cells.

This mutation causes the mechanisms that control cell replication to become non-functional and the mechanisms that encourage cell division to become increased. Therefore the increasing ball of cells has multiple effects including:

- using resources needed for growth and repair in other parts of the body;
- physical effects such as blockages of airways in lung cancer, or bowel motions in colon cancer;
- spread to other parts of the body (metastasis).

133. What cancers do you think we can prevent?

Consider the following four points:

- Cervical cancer can be prevented by a vaccine of the virus causing it (see question 134).
- The chances of getting lung cancer can be greatly reduced by stopping smoking. The ban on the use of asbestos in housing also reduces the chances of getting lung cancer.

- Colon cancer may be reduced by a high-fibre diet.

- Breast cancer is routinely screened for by mammography (X-raying of the breasts) and if treated early can be cured.

134. Why is the HPV vaccine considered by some to be controversial?

The human papilloma virus is one of the main risk factors in the development of cervical cancer. It infects the cells in the cervix and causes both an increased rate of cell reproduction by damaging cells and also damage to the DNA, which predisposes the cells to developing cancer. HPV is transmitted via sexual intercourse. The reason the HPV vaccine is controversial is that it is given to girls under 16 and, therefore, is seen by some to indicate acceptance or tolerance of under-age sex.

135. What does smoking do to you?

Cigarette smoke has the following effects:

- Nicotine binds to receptors on nerves and causes some changes in the way nerve impulses are conducted. It forms the pharmacological basis for the addiction to cigarettes.

- Tar causes paralysation of the ciliated cells that line the airways, which normally move mucus up and out of the airways by waving fine hair-like structures (cilia). This causes mucus to become trapped and infected in the airways, giving rise to chronic bronchitis (long-term inflammation of the airways) and emphysema (dilatation of the alveoli due to breakdown of elastase via inflammatory cells).

- Tar also contains a number of carcinogens, which are chemicals capable of causing direct damage to DNA, resulting in mutations that may give rise to lung cancer.

- Other substances in cigarette smoke are harmful to the lining of the arteries and can increase the chance of suffering a heart attack or stroke.

136. What can drinking too much alcohol do to you?

You can divide this answer up into the short-term and long-term effects.

Short-term effects

- decreased inhibition;

- flushing;

- slurred speech;

- poor coordination;

- impaired decision making;

- in very high overdose, acute liver damage, coma and death.

Long-term effects

- liver disease that ends in cirrhosis (shrinking of the liver);

- increased risk of bleeding from the oesophagus;

- easy bruising – as clotting factors are produced in the liver;

- cerebral atrophy (shrinking of the brain).

137. What are the arguments for and against banning the sale of tobacco?

These are some arguments for a ban:

- Tobacco is known to greatly increase the chances of getting lung cancer, emphysema and bronchitis. Banning it would allow us to reduce the burdens of these diseases on the population.

- There is some evidence of a genetic predisposition to be addicted to cigarettes, therefore we would be protecting individuals who might not wish to smoke.

- There is also some evidence of the harm of secondary smoke, for example harm to those around smokers, and therefore we would be preventing harm to others too. This would decrease the spending required by the NHS on smoking-related diseases.

These are some arguments against a ban:

- The tax on the sale of tobacco generates a large revenue that the government can use to spend on important services such as health care.

- Some would argue that we should be allowed to choose the activities we take part in and the products we consume. Butter, for example, may cause obesity, but it is difficult to imagine a ban on butter or ice-cream just because they can be harmful.

- Banning of unhealthy substances may not result in reduced consumption, as they may become available on the black market, as in the case of illegal drugs.

This would cause further problems as there would be no control on quality. In the case of cigarettes, unscrupulous dealers could mix tobacco with cheaper products, such as sawdust, to maximize profits. Banning smoking could also fuel an increase in black market cigarettes, which might indirectly lead to more crimes to fund a smoking habit.

138. Tell us what Herceptin is. How are very expensive treatments rationed in the UK?

Herceptin is an anti-cancer drug that has been developed to treat breast cancer. When introduced, it was controversial as it was so expensive that it could only be made available to a limited number of patients in the UK.

In the UK, in order to be given an expensive therapy, the following conditions may need to be met:

- The treatment must have a strong evidence base showing its effectiveness.

- Cheaper alternative or 'first-line' therapies should be tried first.

- The comparison between potential candidates may be quantified. One device used for such a calculation is the QALY – quality-adjusted life years – that the patient would gain. This is the number of years the patient is expected to live, multiplied by a modifier that takes into account the quality of life.

Summary

- This chapter contains a vast amount of data, and will take you some time to become fully comfortable with all of it.

- General awareness of medical issues is important so supplement this chapter with reading of news and current affairs on the issues discussed.

- The approach to medical science questions comes from detailed knowledge.

- In addition to these topics, ensure that you undertake detailed reading in any specialities or interests you may have mentioned in your personal statement.

CHAPTER 11

Ethics and law

Introduction

Ethics and law forms a part of the interview for almost all universities, and students often feel confident in answering the questions with little preparation. However, this confidence can be a negative thing, as the answers given are often unipolar, without considering all the complexities of the ethical or legal conundrum being posed. This chapter deals with how to take a balanced and analytical approach to ethical problems, to demonstrate to the interview panel both your knowledge base and your reasoning skills.

Ethics and law

Ethics

Ethics may be defined as a system of moral principles relating to human conduct, with respect to concepts such as right or wrong, justice and virtue. Law is a system of rules relating to human conduct, established and enforced by custom, agreement or authority. There is often a considerable degree of overlap between ethics and law, and laws have ethical principles underlying them, but there can be exceptions where ethics and law are at opposing points of view.

What is the difference between ethics and law? Ethics are not always enforceable, whereas laws are more commonly binding and infringements of them may result in penalties of some description, although this is not always the case. Laws are written by man, and in this country approved by parliament. They are recorded in legislature or case histories. Ethics, on the other hand, can refer to sources outside of mankind such as God, a natural law or fundamental principles.

Ethical questions

Using all or some of the 'four principles' (see below) is one method you can use to analyse ethical problems. The concept is that there are two discrete spectrums the polar ends of which represent extremes of an ethical principle. Take, for example, the autonomy–justice spectrum. At one end lies the principle that we should respect an individual's right to choose what he or she wants, while at the other end lies the principle that we should aim for the greatest happiness for the greatest good. In the case of euthanasia, we have to balance the desire of the patient to end his or her suffering against the risks to the general population of mistakes in euthanasia, and a slippery slope in devaluing human life. Thus, it is important to take both autonomy and justice into consideration when thinking about euthanasia.

These are the four principles:

- Justice – which deals with fair distribution of resources, equality and protection of the innocent.

- Autonomy – which promotes respect for the wishes of an individual.

- Beneficence – which espouses the duty to do good to others.

- Non-maleficence – which is concerned with not doing harm to people.

Law

Admissions tutors will not expect you to be familiar with a whole list of legal cases; you are applying to study medicine after all. However, practising doctors should be aware of the law in several areas, as it will affect their practice. One of the key areas of law is medical negligence, which strikes fear into the heart. Criminal law is rarely applied to doctors in negligence cases unless there are extreme circumstances, and there is the most serious type of charge with the possibility of substantial prison sentences. Therefore, medical negligence falls under the law of tort, which is civil law.

In order to prove a case of negligence, a plaintiff must prove three separate things occurred. If any of these three are absent then the medical practitioner is not guilty of negligence. They are as follows:

- The doctor owed the plaintiff a duty of care.

- The doctor was in breach of his or her duty of care.

- The plaintiff suffered harm as a result.

Remember that tort law is civil law, and as such the degree of proof required is 'on the balance of probabilities' and not 'beyond reasonable doubt'. Nevertheless, it is often hard to prove that any harm suffered by a patient was directly due to the actions of a doctor. However, if the doctor is found guilty, the victim will be awarded damages for pain and suffering, as well as loss of earnings, both previous and future.

Remember that the GMC is another disciplinary body that can reprimand doctors. This is outside of the legal sphere, but provides an independent source of regulation for the practice of medicine. Doctors may be put on a kind of probation, with restrictions on their practice; for example they may be required to be under supervision. They may also be struck off the register, which in essence means not being able to practise medicine again. GMC hearings are usually performed by a panel of doctors, as opposed to a jury in legal cases.

Questions

Consent

139. A man refuses treatment for a potentially life-threatening condition. What are the ethical issues involved?

Four principles analysis raises these issues:

- Justice – resources used to treat an unwilling patient could be better spent on patients who desire active treatment.

- Autonomy – we should respect the patient's right to choose his treatment.

- Beneficence – we should attempt to do patients good whenever we can.

- Non-maleficence – treating the patient against his will may be considered to be doing harm, and particularly from the mental health perspective.

Example answer

'The first consideration is whether or not this man's refusal of the treatment is consistent. The patient may be having a knee-jerk reaction out of fear of the treatment reaction, or the stresses of his condition. It would be reasonable to check if the patient's refusal of treatment

represents his true feelings by discussing the reasons why he is refusing in more depth. The next consideration is whether or not the patient has the capacity to consent to treatment. This involves being able to understand, retain and weigh up the information to come to a balanced conclusion. Things that can reduce a patient's capacity include intoxication, dementia or disability. If the patient is competent, however, we are ethically bound to respect his wishes with regard to treatment. Legally, we are not allowed to treat people against their will as this may be equivalent to assault.'

140. The same man who has previously refused treatment for a life-threatening condition becomes unconscious. How does this change the situation?

The situation will be changed as the man is no longer in a position to express his wishes. Therefore, the man cannot possess the capacity to consent to his treatment, and the judgement must be made in his best interests. In the instances of life-saving or emergency treatment, there is a presumption towards the preservation of life, unless there are very strong reasons for this not to be the case. These reasons might be consistent previous expressed wishes to die or a legal advanced directive with clear written instructions regarding life-threatening illness.

141. Explain how organ donation is currently set up in the UK. Do you think there should be an opt-out system?

Donation from willing people is the source of organs for transplantation operations that can save lives or vastly improve the quality of life of patients. In the UK, there is currently an opt-in system whereby in order to be an organ donor you must sign up to the organ donation register. You may carry a card that states your wish to donate your organs in the event of death.

It is commonly stated that many more people say they would wish to be organ donors than are currently registered and therefore some people propose a system where the 'default' setting is for everyone to be a potential donor, with those who do not wish to take part being able to opt out. An opt-out system may be promoted by the principle of justice, where more people stand to benefit from a donated organ. However, an opt-out system may violate the principle of autonomy, as we should be free to choose what is done to our bodies. There are also other considerations: some religious beliefs promote leaving the human body intact after death; and relatives of the deceased may find it distressing that their loved one's body was to be dissected and used. An opt-in system prevents such violations of autonomy, but reduces the number of overall organs available for transplant.

142. A male patient comes to you with flu-like symptoms two months after starting an extra-marital affair and his HIV test returns as positive. You break the news to him and explain the implications and safety issues. However, he insists that he will continue to have unprotected sex with both his mistress and his wife, who is also a patient under your care. What should you do?

Using some of the four principles (listed earlier in the chapter) raises the following points. The patient's autonomy, in choosing what he wishes to do, comes into conflict with the principle of non-maleficence, specifically in the risk of harming two other people, one of whom is a patient under your care.

Doctor–patient confidentiality is an important principle to maintain, as the trust that is formed is vital for the practice of medicine. Patients may need to tell you intimate or embarrassing details about their bodies and lives in order for you to make a diagnosis, and the knowledge that this information will be kept secret will encourage patients to be more forthcoming. The principle of justice applies here. However, confidentiality can be breached in the following circumstances:

- when there is a statutory requirement, such as informing the driving license agency about a diagnosis of epilepsy;

- if issued with a court order;

- to prevent a serious crime;

- to prevent harm to others.

Example answer

'In the first instance it would be helpful to talk to the patient and try to understand why he wishes to continue his risky behaviour. It would be appropriate to discuss barrier contraceptives such as condoms and other methods to reduce the risk of transmission. However, if the patient cannot be persuaded, then the risk of harm to his wife (infection by a serious, potentially life-shortening disease) would outweigh the risk of harm to the therapeutic relationship, and I would therefore be obliged to tell his wife to protect her health.'

The GMC says 'You may disclose information to a known sexual contact of a patient with HIV where you have reason to think that the patient has not informed that person, and cannot be persuaded to do so.'

143. Define medical negligence for us. Can a doctor go to jail for negligence?

Medical negligence has been described in the section on law above, and involves a duty of care that has been breached, causing harm. Negligence is usually under the premise of civil law, for which the penalties do not include a jail sentence. Payments to the victims are often not borne by the doctors themselves, but by their defence company (legal insurance for practice) or by their employing hospital.

However, very serious cases of negligence can be seen under criminal law, if there has been deliberate omission or planning on the part of the accused, or if there has been negligence to such a degree that it recklessly endangered another's life. In practice this is very rare in the UK.

Confidentiality

144. Would you prescribe the oral contraceptive pill to a 14-year-old girl who is sleeping with her boyfriend? What if her mother objected?

The principle of autonomy may suggest that we should respect the wishes of the girl, but this comes into conflict with the principle of justice, which involves the protection of vulnerable individuals. This may result in a value judgement as to whether the girl is competent to consent to her own treatment if under the age of 14. The test we can apply is known as Gillick competence, after a case where a mother sued a hospital authority for treating her daughter without her mother's consent. The court ruled in favour of the hospital authority, stating that even though the girl was a minor (under 16), she had sufficient intelligence and understanding to understand what was being proposed in terms of treatment. Therefore, if this patient met these criteria, you would also be legally allowed to treat her without her mother's consent.

There is, however, an additional point. Sex with a minor under a certain age is considered statutory rape, and that threshold is 13 years of age in the UK. Therefore you may be obliged to reveal this information to the police to prevent a serious crime – rape.

145. Some people feel that doctors should refuse to perform operations on obese patients. What are the issues involved?

The likelihood of success of some operations can be affected by obesity, and patients may also suffer from more complications such as deep-vein thrombosis. Therefore, in terms of the principle of justice, it could be said that in a system of limited resources, we should favour the patients who have a better chance of success as this would increase the overall benefit from the money spent. This comes into conflict with the principles of autonomy and beneficence, first, as obesity may not be the choice of the patient – he or she could have a metabolic or psychiatric disorder that manifests itself as obesity. Even if it is the patient's choice, should we ignore people who need treatment, simply because they cannot or will not lead a healthier lifestyle?

Other factors, such as the following, may be involved:

- Surgeons may not wish to perform surgery on high-risk patients as it would adversely affect their hospital's mortality and success rates, which could be linked to funding.

- Personal prejudices against obese patients may become involved.

- There may be practical complications, such as the requirement for a reinforced operating table, or scanners large enough to accommodate the patient's body.

146. Should drug companies be allowed to charge so much for their products?

Consider the following points in favour of allowing drug companies to charge high prices:

- Drug companies are businesses, which need to make a profit to survive, and therefore are driven to continue finding new drugs as part of their objectives, which benefits the patients.

- Research is a large branch of investment for drug companies, and therefore the money that they make is in part 'recycled' to benefit another set of patients who can make use of a newly developed drug.

- There are secondary benefits from the economic success such as stimulating the economy and payment of corporate tax.

These points could be made against allowing drug companies to charge high prices:

- It creates a health inequality, particularly for the health services of developing nations.

- It limits the number of people who can benefit from the treatment at the present time.

- In a limited resource system, such as the NHS, it can divert resources away from other essential services and treatments.

147. Should drug companies be allowed to sponsor doctors' meetings and give them free products?

Drug companies often sponsor educational or departmental meetings for doctors. Here are some of the arguments in favour of this:

- Drug companies are not allowed to offer doctors direct financial incentives, or, for example, holidays.

- In the case of educational meetings, doctors should be able to interpret the data of studies themselves, and therefore would not be unduly influenced by drug company presentations as they view them in the light of the results of other studies.

- Other companies that produce consumer products are allowed free licence to advertise and therefore pharmaceutical companies should be allowed to do likewise.

Here are some of the arguments against this practice:

- The principle of 'bribery' is still valid, even if the quantitative nature is small.

- Drug companies may be able to influence unduly the prescribing patterns of doctors in this manner.

- It is difficult to draw the line between what constitutes reasonable advertising and promotion, and what is slightly underhand.

Resource allocation

148. Should alternative or complementary medicine be funded by the NHS, and why?

Consider these issues. The basis for approval of treatments of the NHS is efficacy and value for money. These are assessed by NICE (the National Institute for Health and Clinical Excellence) and decisions are made to fund or not fund treatments, which are published as NICE guidelines. One of the key factors is whether or not there is strong evidence that a therapy actually works, and in practice this is established by clinical trials. These are experiments in which the therapy under question is compared against placebos and alternative medications.

You might say you are not sure what the trial data show, but if the treatment is proven to be effective then it should be funded as for any other treatment, giving a good differential manifestation. This process of selecting medication policy by data is known as evidence-based medicine and is an important part of practising modern medicine. Keeping up to date with the evidence for treatment is important for every clinician.

149. Should international aid organizations such as Médecins Sans Frontières (MSF) take a political stance?

One of the mission statements of MSF is that in addition to providing medical care when needed, it should bear witness and raise political awareness of the suffering of the people it helps. This sounds like a laudable ideal but may involve some complications as well.

These are some arguments for international aid organizations taking a political stance:

- It is of immediate benefit to the sufferers of a conflict crisis as it may raise political awareness and stimulate efforts towards ending the conflict. There may also be indirect benefit, for example by inspiring people to donate to direct fund-raising appeals, raising more funds for aid efforts.

- It forms a longer-term protection for the suffering population if there is international awareness of the plight. International intervention may prevent conflict-based suffering of a similar type, therefore helping to secure the present and immediate future as well.

- It is helpful as a world community to see the suffering of others, so that we can help if we are so inclined, and learn what might be causing it. If we are not aware, we cannot make this choice to help or ignore.

These are some of the arguments against such organizations taking a political stance:

- In areas of human conflict, parties may allow totally impartial aid organizations, but not, for example, the media. If an aid organization functions essentially as both, it may be that the people it is trying to help are denied access to medical treatment on the basis of their public position to report on what is being undertaken.

- There are other specialist agencies that deal with reporting of information impartially to the world. It is therefore inefficient to use aid doctors and medical staff in this capacity which may detract from their overall clinical work.

- It may be difficult to remain truly impartial, and the socio-economic, cultural and geographical make-up of an aid organization contingent may affect the nature of the reporting that occurs. This point may be true of all agencies, but there is no reason to assume that doctors would be more impartial than any other reporters, particularly as they are exposed first-hand to the victims of a conflict and may be affected by a visceral reaction to blood and suffering, and be in a less optimal position to deliver an objective assessment.

> If you have mentioned a desire to work for an international aid organization, be well prepared to discuss not only what the aims of such organizations are, but what you think of them.

150. Should the NHS fund the treatment of self-inflicted diseases?

Let us return to three of the principles used in four principles analysis to consider this.

- Autonomy – there is an argument that we should be free to choose our activities, and not be penalized as a result of them as long as they are not harming others. It could be argued that since some harmful activities such as smoking are addictive, and we understand the underlying neurobiological mechanism by which this occurs, there is less 'fault' than we think and some people may be more a victim of genetics than their own behaviour.

- Justice – we should optimize the use of our resources and therefore it may be true that treating smokers who suffer from, for example, heart disease may be less successful than treating non-smokers, and therefore a less-efficient use of precious funds.

- Beneficence – this principle implies a duty to treat all suffers of a disease regardless of the cause.

If people wish to continue their dangerous activities, it may be possible to dissuade them via financial incentives, for example charging higher health insurance premiums. This would offset the financial loss from an increase in demand for treatment. However, as the NHS provides health care free of charge at time of delivery, this is not possible in the UK at present.

151. Should we treat patients for emphysema or heart disease who continue to smoke?

Many students have reported being asked this question, and they have found it links on from a scientific discussion regarding the particular disease in question. Many of the approaches in previous questions (particularly question 150) would be appropriate here, along with these points. Sufferers of heart disease who continue to smoke are more likely to suffer from repeat problems than those who do not. Therefore, we can use secondary prevention measures (preventing an event from occurring again) by, for example, giving aspirin after a patient has a heart attack, to affect the clotting system in the blood and reduce the risk of forming a thrombus (clot in the blood vessel supplying the heart). Similarly, in smokers with lung problems, active treatment may reduce the cost of the disease burden in terms of hospitalizations of patients once they reach a critical condition.

> These points illustrate a good integration of both ethical points and medical knowledge, which may be helpful if the question is asked following on from a scientific discussion.

152. Suggest how funding health care using a system based on health insurance might be better than the NHS. What would be the problems?

One advantage of such a system could be efficiency. Any competitive system increases efficiency and decreases costs, and health insurance companies would have to compete with each other for business in terms of cheapest premiums with best coverage. Another advantage would be targeted distribution of cost; that is, the people who use the health service most would be the ones paying the most for it.

The main problems would be as follows:

● Health–wealth inequalities – lower socio-economic groups might not be able to afford insurance, giving rise to a divide in the health care of the population based on wealth.

● Health neglect – patients may wish to save money to spend on other things, and therefore knowingly neglect their health.

● Health discrimination – those with certain conditions, for example genetic disorders such as cystic fibrosis, may require more frequent hospitalizations. Therefore, insurance companies might charge them higher premiums based purely on their condition or genetic make-up.

153. What would be the benefits of legalizing currently illegal drugs and what would be the pitfalls?

Benefits would include:

● government regulation;

● tax revenues;

- monitoring of drug use;

- reduction in crime;

- reduction in the illicit appeal of the substances as they become more mainstream.

The measure would have the following pitfalls:

- It may suggest endorsement of the substances as acceptable.

- It would not remove the side-effects of taking the drugs.

- The drugs would be more readily usable as a method of suicide, as they would be legally available.

Abortion

154. What is the law regarding abortion in the UK?

Abortion in the UK is legalized under the 1967 Abortion Act, under the following circumstances:

- up to 24 weeks gestation, if there is a greater risk of harm to the physical or mental health of the mother by continuing the pregnancy;

- at any time if there is a grave risk of serious harm to the mother;

- if the foetus is likely to be born with severe physical or mental abnormalities.

> In practice, there will always be a greater risk to the mother in terms of mental or physical health as even the act of giving birth has some associated risks. Therefore, before 24 weeks, abortion can be sought by almost anyone provided the woman is worried about the harm (including mental or emotional distress) that would be caused by continuing the pregnancy.

155. Would you perform abortions as a doctor?

This question asks you as a student a personally directed question and it is easy to dive in with a 'yes' or 'no' answer. Remember to give arguments for and against abortion before giving your own opinion in a balanced conclusion.

Taking two of the four principles used earlier, the conflict is essentially between the right of the mother to control what is done to, and in, her own body (autonomy), versus the protecting of an innocent life (justice). The question of whether an embryo is a life or not is a complicated one and forms the basis of much of the controversy surrounding abortion. Some consider the fertilized egg to be a life at the moment of fertilization, others not until the baby has emerged from the body and others still not until the foetus is capable of surviving outside the womb by itself.

You may wish to consider the special situations of:

● abortion in a victim of rape;

● abortion of a child with a severe and incurable genetic defect;

● abortion of a child in a very young mother.

> Doctors are allowed to 'conscientiously object' to referring a patient for an abortion. However, they cannot obstruct a patient from seeking such an intervention, and must refer her to an appropriate colleague or department to meet her needs.

Fertility

156. Explain what human rights are. What human rights do you know and how are they enforced?

Human rights are the rights and freedoms to which all humans are entitled, by virtue of being human. You may wish to discuss:

● the right to life;

● the right not to be tortured;

● the right not to be enslaved;

● the right to a fair trial;

● the right to freedom of thought and religion;

● the right to freedom of expression;

● the right to marriage and a family life.

In terms of enforcement, in the UK the European Convention on Human Rights gives details many of such rights, and violations of these rights can be challenged under EU law. Internationally, it is up to the international community at large to enforce application of human rights and to punish those who deny others these rights; this is most functionally seen in actions taken by the UN.

157. What are the issues involved in in-vitro fertilization?

In-vitro fertilization is a process by which eggs are taken from the ovaries of a parent and sperm are directly injected into it for fertilization. It is controversial owing to its relatively poor success rate and high expense, costing in the tens of thousands of pounds.

These are the main issues, which relate to three of the four principles:

- Justice – the expense and poor success rate of this treatment can be difficult to justify when compared to other life-saving treatments. It is also not healing a direct illness that makes a patient unable to go about daily life, and many people choose not to have children and are not harmed by that choice.

- Autonomy – do we have a right to have children if we want to? If so, does this imply a right to have assistance if we are unable to conceive naturally?

- Beneficence – if we can help those unable to conceive but who wish to, we are doing a good deed for them. This may also relieve the stresses that can occur between couples as a result of fertility issues.

Adoption of children is another valid option to consider in cases of infertility.

End of life issues

158. What is your feeling about euthanasia?

The word euthanasia comes from the Greek for 'good death' and involves active killing of a patient who wishes to die, because of extreme pain or a terminal condition.

Four principles analysis raises these points:

- Non-maleficence – 'First do no harm'. We may have to consider the potential harm not only to the patient, but to others based on the so-called 'slippery slope' argument. This argument is based on the principle that if we allow the mercy killing of people in pain, we are weakening the sanctity of human life. It would open the doorway to kill people who had handicaps, diseases or perhaps even ideologies that we thought were negative. It also risks the possibility of age discrimination and pressure for euthanasia on the elderly.

- Beneficence – we could consider euthanasia to be doing good for the patient if there is no other way to relieve intolerable suffering.

- Justice – from the utilitarian perspective, it might be beneficial to let those who truly wish to end their life die. That way, they would be satisfied with the outcome, as well as freeing up valuable resources for those left behind.

- Autonomy – we should respect the right of the individual to make decisions concerning what to do with his or her life, even if it involves the individual's death.

> If you are considering a pro-euthanasia position, it is important to make sure that the wish to die is a consistent one. Patients might say the pain is so bad that if they had a gun they would shoot themselves, but this can be a transient feeling that is being expressed.

Medical research

159. Should animal testing be used in medical research?

These are the issues raised by four principles analysis:

- Justice – the animals are not benefiting from the research themselves and therefore are being used as a means to an end. The suffering and death of animals for the benefit of humans can be considered unfair on the part of the sufferers.

- Beneficence – the results of animal research may be very beneficial. Other than just treatments and cures, it may well improve our understanding of science in general, from physiology to neuroscience to pharmacology, and thereby expand the boundaries of our knowledge.

- Non-maleficence – the principle of not doing harm comes into conflict with animal research as we are actively and deliberately taking part in the harm of living creatures.

- Autonomy – do we as a species have the right to do as we please with regard to other species? Or do they also have their own autonomy?

On balance, the cost–benefit analysis may be summed up as follows: the benefit to us humans in terms of treatments for our illnesses must be paid by a cost to our humanity by actively sanctioning the suffering and death of animals. Whether or not this is a justifiable cost hinges on our perception of animals as compared to humans.

If they are considered less than human, for reasons such as not having a 'soul', then indeed it may be worth the suffering of many animals to ease the suffering of humans with a disease. If we treat ourselves as one species out of the animal kingdom, we may abhor the suffering associated with research, even with its potential benefits to our own kind.

Another point to consider is that it may be that our objection to animal research is visceral – we have a tendency to have a 'gut' reaction to pain, blood, suffering and death. This may cloud our judgement as to the actual facts of the matter.

160. Trials of new medications involve risk to the health of individuals and can result in serious injury or death. How can we justify this?

Consider these points:

● Autonomy – participants of medical trials are theoretically free to choose to take part, knowing the risks and rewards of their undertaking. There are often monetary rewards to taking part, and as many people like to gamble, should we not allow them to take a risk for the gain of money, even if that risk is associated with physical rather than financial harm?

● Non-maleficence – putting healthy people in harm's way seems like the opposite of what the medical profession is trying to achieve. There may be a quantitative relationship here. We may accept the harming of a handful of people in the pursuit of a cure that will affect thousands. However, would we be willing to accept the harm of 100 people? Or 1,000?

● Beneficence – we must balance the risk for the trial participants with the good the research will do for the health of the population as a whole. The benefit of evidence-based medicine and modern pharmaceuticals depends on robust medical research and clinical trials. Considering the problem in reverse, we could also be seen as doing good to the population by trialling medications before the general approval of a drug, as if there is an adverse reaction, we are confining that harm to the trial participants only, thereby preventing harm to the rest of the population.

On balance, utilitarianism ethics might advocate the greatest good for the greatest number, but from the deontological perspective, we may be seen to be using the trial participants as a means to an end. Overall, however, we should consider that the value of trial data in medical research has implications not only for the current generations of suffers of a disease, but future generations too, whereas the harm will be limited to the participants.

Conscripted harm may be less palatable, but recruiting volunteers and rewarding them for the risk undertaken may be more acceptable. However, we must take into account the fact that the socio-economically disadvantaged would be more inclined to undertake the risk, giving rise to a health inequality for economic reasons.

Child issues

161. If you were the doctor working in accident and emergency, and a parent brought in a child with burn marks that looked suspiciously like cigarette burns, what should you do?

This question deals with the difficulties of reporting suspected child abuse. There have been high-profile cases in the media, such as that of 'Baby P' who was a 17-month-old baby who died of repeated injuries inflicted over an eight-month period by his mother and her boyfriend. Baby P was seen repeatedly in NHS health services by doctors, as well as social workers, but not enough was done to save his life. Take a balanced approach to this question based on four principles analysis. The two main principles at play are justice and non-maleficence.

In terms of justice, we must take into account the safety of the child, and our need to protect vulnerable individuals in our society. If there is a genuine cause for concern, we should do all in our power to see that it is investigated or call for help from those with the power and expertise to do more about it. This may involve social services or the police.

The non-maleficence principle applies when we consider falsely accusing a parent or carer of child abuse. It would already be traumatizing for parents innocent of abuse to witness their child suffering, and it would be doubly so if they were falsely accused of being the cause. It is therefore important that your accusations are based on some material evidence or genuine suspicion, in order to prevent the harm associated with such error in accusation.

On balance, if you have any reason to be suspicious, it may be wise to consult a peer or senior colleague about what he or she makes of the case. If there are suspicions, you could ask the parents or carers for more details about the incidents causing the injury, which could reveal some inconsistencies in their story. If you are not convinced either way, it may be appropriate to inform social services or child protection agencies that there is a possibility of child abuse, such that the safety of your patient is placed as your top priority.

Other ethical and legal points to consider are as follows:

- The medical notes for a legal document, and therefore careful notation of information surrounding the incident, which may include taking photographs of the wounds, should be undertaken. You should also record your discussions with the parents.

- There is now a requirement to have a doctor designated for child protection in hospitals, who can be consulted in cases of suspected child abuse. You may also wish to consult a senior colleague if you are unsure of what to do.

- The GMC recommends that you should participate fully in child abuse investigations, including requests for information from appropriate agencies.

162. Should people be allowed to sell one of their kidneys if they wish?

Consider the following points in favour of allowing this:

- Autonomy – humans are allowed to sell their time in terms of work and manual labour, and this may at times pose a risk to their health. Wig-makers can also buy human hair for their products. Therefore we should respect the wishes of the individual.

- Physiology – humans usually only require the functional capacity of one kidney in order to survive, and therefore it is not of great importance to maintain two kidneys unless there is a problem with them.

- If patients do develop problems with their one remaining kidney, it will be easier for them to find a replacement if the selling of kidneys is legal.

- It would ensure that all transactions would be regulated and performed by registered surgeons.

Here are some arguments against allowing this:

- People in lower socio-economic classes may be pressured into selling a kidney, more so than the higher classes. This would generate a health inequality based on wealth.

- Some people suffer from a disease that limits their kidney function and may require them to have both kidneys. This might include conditions such as polycystic kidney disease, which is an inherited disease causing the kidneys to develop many fluid-filled sacs (cysts).

- It would expose many people to the risks of surgery in general, such as the general anaesthetic and risk of infection.

Further reading

http://www.gmc-uk.org/guidance

This website contains detailed guidance on ethical and legal problems faced in a career in medicine, and is used by practising doctors. Keeping in line with the policies of the GMC is a good way to avoid disciplinary issues or legal problems and for students it provides a good basis for revision.

Summary

- You are not expected to become a lawyer, but the key cases may be useful in explaining your point and will impress admissions tutors with your breadth of knowledge.

- Ethical problems are usually amenable to analysis using some or all of the four principles, which can be used to demonstrate your awareness of how practising doctors may approach problems.

- Avoid giving answers that are unipolar, as there are inevitably different viewpoints on ethical issues.

- Try to summarize the arguments for and against a particular proposition before concluding with your own answer, as this will give a balanced and reasoned approach.

CHAPTER 12

International students

Introduction

International students have to contend with a special group of competitors – other international students. The competition ratios will be steep, as most medical schools have a maximum quota of international intake, which is coupled with a larger supply of applicants from around the globe. By sheer economics, if you are an international student this equation leaves you facing a more demanding situation than local students.

Several admissions tutors admit that they 'love international students' as they tend to be very diligent and talented. International students may be faced with a single interviewer if their interview is conducted in their home country.

The main advice for international students wishing to be successful in their medical school interview is this: focus hard on learning the material, skills and techniques from the other chapters in this book. It is on these grounds that you should seek to outdo your peers and, in particular, if language is not your strong point you should focus on grammar, relevant vocabulary and most importantly structuring your answers when preparing for interview. Many candidates spend a great deal of time on superficial communication issues such as body language and accent; and while these are good additions to a package, having a well-balanced structured answer with good content will always triumph over a rambling answer expressed in the Queen's English.

This chapter covers some of the questions that have been regularly posed to international students. International students facing an Oxbridge interview should note that the majority of the interview will be on scientific and academic questions, and should spend most of their time preparing for the type of questions and processes seen in Chapter 14.

Questions

163. How do you feel about the prospect of studying in the UK?

Several students have reported having this question early on in their interview and finding it difficult, as it is asking them to describe feelings rather than concrete facts. However, you can refer to the following advantages and disadvantages of studying in the UK in your answer.

Some advantages are:

- Studying in a new country will be stimulating and challenging, which will aid your drive to succeed.

- Exposure to a new environment will necessitate the development of inter-personal communication skills that will build a strong foundation for future doctor–patient interactions.

- A lack of reliance on previous support networks will force you to be an independent learner and person in general, which will be a helpful trait in your career as a doctor.

Now consider these disadvantages:

- Lack of familiarity with local processes – this might affect logistical affairs such as transport and budget planning.

- Language difficulties – you may find the variety of accents difficult to interpret at first.

- Unfamiliarity with colloquialisms – you may find that wordplay, sarcasm and humour function differently from in your own country and this may make it harder for you in social settings to start off with.

- Physiology – you may take some time to become adjusted to the UK's weather if it is significantly different from that in your home country.

You can qualify these disadvantages by stating that they are mostly temporary in nature, and with stoic tolerance and a keenness to adapt, you will be able to overcome them.

Example answer

'I think the best way to describe my feelings is as a combination of enthusiasm, excitement and anxiety. I wouldn't be honest if I didn't say I was a little bit anxious about moving away from my comfort zone and experiencing a foreign environment, and even though I have consulted with seniors about what to expect in terms of the course, peers and country, I think it is hard to know for sure until I am really there. I feel that this anxiety is balanced by excitement, which comes from the prospect of experiencing a new culture and making new acquaintances; and improving my language skills is a large appeal. However, my enthusiasm is mainly based around the new challenges of studying to become a doctor, particularly in a foreign environment. If I studied more locally, I might be tempted to rely on my family and friends from school and so by coming abroad I will force myself to adapt, learn and be proactive in my academic and social life and I hope gain the resolve and the maturity that comes with it. That is why I am excited about the prospect of studying in the UK.'

Points to note

This candidate demonstrates to the interviewer that he is taking an informed approach in discussions with seniors and has put considerable thought into both the pros and cons of his future study plans.

164. Can you give any examples that demonstrate your independence?

Consider the following:

- Activities under minimal supervision, such as initiating a new school club or society.

- Activities that have required a residential element such as a summer school or army service.

- Activities that involve independent learning, such as courses or reading outside of your school curriculum, or developing a special interest in a subject.

- Utilize the principles of DPT to create an engaging experience for the interviewers.

165. What are the differences in health care between the NHS and the system in (your home country)?

You will need to know about what the NHS is, what its aims are and how it functions. For these details, refer to questions 89, 90 and 91.

Depending on your home country, there may be an insurance scheme where there are hospitals for people who work for certain companies or for the government. There may be a discounted health care system whereby a small fee will cover the cost of all medical treatments.

Here are some things to research:

- How is secondary (hospital) care funded and supplied in your country?

- How is primary care (GP, community medicine) funded and delivered in your country?

- What role does private practice play in your country?

- How do medical training and medical careers in your country differ from those in the UK?

Consider the advantages and disadvantages of both systems and be prepared to deliver a balanced and reasoned argument for this question.

166. How will you cope with being away from your support networks?

This question encourages students to think ahead to the situation they will arrive in, and to demonstrate that they have. It also requires them to have researched and considered the social, as well as academic, element of studying at university.

Consider the following points:

- Many universities have international student societies that offer support, advice and a place to meet fellow students.

- Modern technology such as the internet will allow good contact with parents and friends back home.

- You may wish to reference previous stays overseas or at other placements.

It can be helpful to take a prospective position for this question, eg to mention that humans are adaptable and forming new support networks is an important social experience.

167. What difficulties do you think are faced by students studying in a language that is not their first language?

Consider the following:

- At medical school you may find that lectures are difficult to follow. There may be literary or popular culture references that you are not familiar with, which can be confusing or distracting.

- You may have to deal with UK patients with their variety of accents and colloquial phrases. This may make it difficult for you to understand them until you become accustomed to it. Conversely, some patients may find you difficult to understand if your accent is particularly strong.

- Prejudice might be an issue. Although in general the country is tolerant of foreigners, you may encounter racism or prejudice on the job, from patients and/or in your day-to-day life. There are support initiatives in both hospitals and medical schools to prevent this but it is an unpleasant reality to which you may be exposed.

Summary

- Preparation for studying in the UK requires careful forethought on the difficulties one might face.

- Talking to current students and doctors in the UK can be the first port of call for this.

- You may find useful information on the International Students website for the university.

- Reading up on current NHS issues may be particularly useful in discussions at interview.

- Reflect on activities you have undertaken that can demonstrate your independence.

CHAPTER 13

Graduate students

Introduction

Graduate students face the difficult task of convincing interviewers of their genuine desire to study medicine. This is often made easier by the fact that for graduate students the desire to study medicine may either be better informed, or more organically developed, than undergraduate applicants' desire. However, the advantages over undergraduates are purely theoretical – as a graduate student you will be competing against candidates who are on par with yourself; that is, they will have the academic background of a degree.

Their degree may give them some insight into a medical career. However, admissions tutors have commented that students of non-medicine related degrees, such as computer science or classics, are often highly motivated and well rounded, and go on to perform well in medical school. Therefore, the actual nature of your degree is not considered to be either an advantage or disadvantage. What tutors are interested in is what you, as a person, gained from your degree and university as a whole. Therefore, the questions that graduate students are asked in addition to the standard inventory typically relate to the subjects and research, teaching and dedication. These are all generic to almost all degrees and this chapter demonstrates how best to utilize your degree experience at interview.

Questions

168. How will your degree be useful to you in your career in medicine?

You can divide the answer into generic skills and medicine-specific skills. In generic skills, you may wish to comment on communication skills, learning in a university environment, analytical and deductive skills. Medicine-specific skills may include a knowledge base, eg cellular biology, as well as research skills and reading scientific literature.

For non-medically related degrees consider your transferable skills, such as communication skills, scientific writing; and your intellectual interest – this addresses the academic component of selection for admissions tutors.

169. What made you decide to switch career paths?

Describe your individual story, detailing the choices you made and why, and how your experiences as well as intellectual interest led you to consider a career as a doctor.

Avoid insulting or being derogatory to your current career or subject choice, as this may reflect poorly on your professional or intellectual integrity. Instead, try to focus on a balanced presentation, comparing your current occupation to what you know about medicine as a subject and career.

170. Do you have any teaching experience?

If you do not have any formal teaching roles, you may still have had some experiences to refer to, such as informally supervising or advising juniors, or simply taking questions from them.

If you have had a teaching role, you may be able to discuss lesson planning, communication skills, improving your own learning by mastering the material and dealing with groups.

> In your answer, you can refer to the fact that teaching plays an important role in medicine. At all levels of seniority doctors are involved in teaching medical students on the wards, and it is important in the continuing professional development of a doctor. Consultants will teach registrars, registrars will teach junior doctors and so on.

171. Do you have any experience with research that you can tell us about?

Research plays an important role in life as a doctor. Studying medicine requires an understanding of the principles of evidence-based practice, clinical trials as well as laboratory sciences, which may reveal the molecular and physiological basis of diseases and treatment.

In answer to this question you may wish to refer to the following:

- Experience of working with statistics can be helpful in planning and interpreting research.

- Laboratory experience may be helpful in understanding techniques.

- Literature review of a subject may have taught you how to navigate online databases.

172. Why did you not choose to study medicine as an undergraduate?

Graduate students often find this the most difficult question to answer. Some of the approaches you may wish to consider include:

- The student was undecided at the point of choosing a degree, and took a course to further their interest in another subject whilst making up their mind. It is quite reasonable for a person of school age not to have decided, and when supported by some objective evidence of a continuing or building interest in medicine, this can be quite compelling.

- A desire for a change in profession after some time in employment – this answer may focus on the differences and similarities between medicine and their current job, and why a career as a doctor is ideal for them, including a discussion of their interests and skills.

- An experience on the degree course undertaken by the student.

Summary

- Developing a narrative for why you wanted to study medicine is important in explaining your unique story to the interview panel.

- Be prepared to discuss your subject or research in considerable depth.

- As well as content, consider the transferable skills learned from your degree.

- Reflect on any employment or long-term commitments, and be able to describe them.

- Graduate interviews require a similar background knowledge base to standard applications, so don't forget to revise the other chapters in the book thoroughly.

CHAPTER 14

Oxbridge

Introduction

Oxbridge interviews are surrounded by a mystique that has confounded and frightened students for years. If you are applying for Oxbridge, you will find that the focus of the questions is almost entirely on testing your scientific knowledge, but more importantly your application of this knowledge to situations you will not be familiar or comfortable with. It therefore goes without saying that in preparation for your interview you should revise carefully your school materials and subjects in science.

One of the main concerns that applicants have surrounds being asked very unusual questions to which they do not seem to know the answers. This chapter will break down these most challenging questions into three types and allow you to develop skills that will allow you not only to answer the questions with fluency and skill, but also to show a desire to seek out more. Some complex ethics problems are also included. This chapter will also give you the knowledge you will require to answer questions regarding the university itself, the course and your motivation to get into your college of choice.

There are three distinct types of questions that you might be faced with during your interview. The first is the 'guesstimate' type, which involves a puzzle to determine something that you have no way of being able to answer accurately, for example 'How many footballs can you fit into an aeroplane?', and can be solved by using approximate and reasoned figures. The second is the explanation type, such as 'Can you tell me about drowning?', and requires you to use your existing knowledge to figure out what might be going on in the question. The third and often most challenging type is the experimental design type, such as 'How would you weigh your own head?', and requires an excellent understanding of statistics, principles of experimental data and confounding factors, as well as the ability to think 'outside of the box'. Questions about motivation for medicine, personal attributes and so on occur much less frequently than in other interviews, but may still feature, so prepare for them using the techniques noted in previous chapters.

Questions

173. Why are you applying to Oxford (or Cambridge)?

Know about the Oxbridge course and the difference between it and other courses. The level of teaching is different, in that you will be given two-to-one small-group teaching, typically for each subject that you take. You will automatically progress to an intercalated degree in your third year. It is possible to do many different subjects, including in-depth study into a particular area of medicine that interests you. Laboratory work is one option – you should consider this if you are possibly interested in pursuing a career in medical research. There is an option to take on an MB PhD programme whereupon you intercalate a PhD into your medicine course, taking it to nine years but qualifying with an impressive combination of PhD and Bachelor of Medicine and Surgery, as well as a BA.

The undergraduate course features in-depth teaching on anatomy, physiology, biochemistry, pathology, pharmacology and neuroscience, with little patient contact. It is also intellectually demanding. The last three years of the course are clinically based. There is a focus on ward shadowing and also on integrated communication skills throughout the course using simulated actors and video analysis.

One of the other features is the collegiate system, which operates such that your education through lectures is delivered through the medical school, but your small-group teaching takes place at your college, which also provides your accommodation and pastoral care. Sports, activities, social events and dining also occur within colleges.

The key features are:

- excellent coverage of the basic sciences underpinning medicine;

- a very wide choice of third-year subjects, including non-medical subjects such as physics and engineering;

- small-group teaching on a two-to-one basis;

- the university's tradition.

The disadvantage is that there is very little or no patient contact in the first three years of the course.

In considering your answer to this question, think through the various advantages of the course. You may find it helpful to phrase these in a positive light, for example 'I am looking forward to in-depth study of the basic sciences underpinning medicine, as an extension of my interest in school-level biology and chemistry,' rather than 'I don't really like the sound of problem-based learning, it sounds rather fluffy, so I preferred Oxford.'

174. Why are you applying to this college?

In terms of selecting a college, there are some broad considerations that you can take into account such as location and size. Other considerations include whether or not you would prefer to be in a smaller college which has a more intimate or family-like social dynamic, and people get to know each other well, or a large college with the opportunity to meet many different people. You might be after specific activities that are strong in certain colleges such as rowing or rugby, and again some research will reveal the answer. Don't forget that these are important, but peripheral, activities as far as the admissions tutors are concerned, so make sure you demonstrate that you are there to study first and foremost.

'Guesstimate'

'Guesstimate' questions involve a puzzle to determine something that you have no way of being able to answer accurately, for example 'How many footballs can you fit into an aeroplane?' You certainly will not know this answer off the top of your head. Many perplexed students will be stunned for some time, and blurt out a random guess. Others will vent their frustration saying 'How can I be expected to answer that?' However, the method to tackling such questions is to use them as an opportunity to show the interviewers your current level of knowledge, and use application and deduction to estimate an answer.

One important element of answering such questions is to materialize the unknown quantities as best you can. This method is demonstrated in the first question below.

175. How many footballs can you fit into an aeroplane?

This seems like a difficult question at first, but the knowledge you will need in order to answer it is relatively basic. If you do not know the answer, try and think of some information that you can use to approximate the data. For example, a football is a sphere, and a plane might be modelled as a cylinder. You may know these volumes from GCSE mathematics to be $\pi R^2 H$ for a cylinder and $4/3\,\pi R^3$ for a sphere. You will also need to volunteer estimates for the answers at this point. It is no good simply stating that you know these formulae, what the examiner is looking for is for you to solve the problem by entering approximate values for the objects.

Example answer

'I know that a football is a sphere and a plane can be modelled as a cylinder. A football is around 20 cm in diameter, and the volume of a sphere is $4/3\,\pi R^3$. The volume of a cylinder is πR^2 times height, and a plane would be approximately 50 metres long and three metres high, giving 353.3 cubed. Therefore, 353.3 cubed divided by 0.033 gives us a total of approximately 10,500 footballs that we could fit into the aeroplane.'

Points to note

This demonstrates your core knowledge of science, which is an important but not sufficient attribute for successful applicants. It then goes on to test your application of this knowledge in a situation that you would not ordinarily be familiar with.

176. How much water is there in a horse?

This question functions in a similar manner to the previous one. The assumed knowledge that you will need is even less than before, and you can draw upon the fact that the human body is approximately 70 per cent water. You could estimate that land mammals might have a similar percentage body composition of water. If you estimate the weight of an adult horse to be 200 kg, 70 per cent of that mass would be 140 kg. Water's density is 1 litre per kg, which gives 140 litres in a horse.

It is important to add 'qualifying statements' to your argument to make it valid. For example, it would not be correct to say that 'humans are 70 per cent water, therefore cows are also' because that is not necessarily true. It is reasonable to argue, however, that 70 per cent is a good estimate based on the fact that both animals are land mammals. Since the interview panel will be looking for your thinking process, as well as your answer, you must take your time to think carefully about the statements you are making.

As always, you should be intellectually cautious, and note the shortcomings with your chosen model. For example, you could state that the composition of a horse might differ significantly from a human, because of differences in the biology. If you demonstrate the qualities of good background knowledge, good application, intellectual caution and awareness of limitation, all with enthusiasm, you may win over the good grace of the interview panel to wish to teach you further.

177. How many animals did Noah take on the Ark?

This question requires you to estimate the number of different species of animals, and multiply the result by two (one male and one female of each). As always in guesstimate type questions, you must volunteer an estimate in order for the question to work. Do not worry if it is not exactly correct, as unless it is grossly mistaken, it will allow you to demonstrate your working. The worst type of answer would be 'I don't know' without any reasoning. If you do happen to guess incorrectly, your answer may well be guided by the interview panel, and be prepared to integrate other information that you now, as well as to learn from the feedback offered by the interviewers themselves.

Points to consider:

- The animal kingdom can be divided into two groups: invertebrates (those without backbones) and vertebrates (those with backbones).

- The majority of species are insects.

- You may wish to mention the categories you are excluding, such as fish, birds etc, as they may nor have required inclusion on board the Ark on the basis that they can swim or fly.

- Current scientific estimates would be between 3 million and 30 million species. This would mean between 6 million and 60 million animals.

A caveat that one student suggested is that if Noah had had more advanced warning, in time to build a bigger ark, he would have been best off taking a ratio of two females to one male. This would allow the repopulation of the earth to be undertaken faster (double the rate) for only an additional increase of 50 per cent loading capacity. This would be more important in animals at the bottom of the food pyramid, so you might choose to bring two female cows and one male cow, but only one female and one male tiger, so that the rate of production of offspring would more closely mirror the ecological demand in terms of herbivore to carnivore ratio. Therefore, he took his estimate of the number of animals, and said that Noah would have taken two times this number, but really should have taken around 2.5 times given these conditions. This kind of additional statement can add value and demonstrate good knowledge and application of the knowledge of biology, as well as bringing in concepts from other disciplines, and the answer was very well received. Try to see if you can incorporate the importance of mathematical relationships if it is relevant.

178. Is hell exothermic or endothermic?

Although this looks like a ferociously difficult question, make use of the information and wording of the question to try and guess which academic discipline to draw upon. Question 176 used 'cow' and 'water' to allude to biology, and 'exothermic' and 'endothermic' should point you towards chemistry. State your knowledge first, and then go on to develop your argument.

Example answer

'Hell is commonly depicted as being "fire and brimstone", which would indicate that there are active chemical reactions of combustion being undertaken. These reactions are exothermic, with the energy released from the breaking of the bonds of the combusting substrate. However, we cannot assume that hell is exothermic simply because these reactions are going on, as they may be needed to maintain the heat in an overall endothermic environment. For example, the rate of heat loss may exceed the rate of production of heat from this combustion. As to where the heat might go, if hell is deep underground in the centre of the earth, it may be lost into the magma underneath the Earth's crust, and used up by, for example, geothermal energy power stations. It may also go to other locations such as purgatory. Therefore, although the presence of combustion reactions suggests an exothermic environment, we cannot be sure that hell is not endothermic without considering the possible routes of heat loss.'

Alternative example answer

'According to Boyle's Law, if the rate of moles entering hell is greater than the rate of expansion of hell, then it will be exothermic. Therefore if we model hell as a finite space, and the souls entering it as moles, if the rate of souls entering hell is greater than the rate of its expansion, it will be exothermic. This means that hell will also be exothermic if it is of a fixed size as there should be a steady stream of souls entering it. However, if hell is an expanding space, and its rate of expansion is greater than the influx of souls, it would be endothermic.'

179. How high can I climb having eaten only a banana?

The previous two questions have alluded to biology and chemistry explanations in turn, and this question is an example involving physics. Physics allows us to relate energy, work done and power and is often useful in simple calculations or estimation of worldly events.

In this case, first you would need to estimate the amount of energy contained in a banana. You may wish to point out that although most energy values that people are concerned about are given in kilocalories, the best unit for relating energy to work done is the kilojoule, and there might be approximately 500 kilojoules in a banana. You would then estimate the mass of the person, and state that the gain in gravitational potential energy is equivalent to mass × gravity × height, which would give the equation:

Energy = MGH
500,000 = 50 × 10 × H (estimating the mass of yourself to be 50kg)
500,000/500 = H
H = 200 metres

For thoroughness, this would be the maximum height you can climb having eaten only a banana. You would then need to subtract estimated losses for many processes such as inefficient absorption in the gut, inefficient transfer to body cells, energy cost for maintaining essential body functions such as cerebral function and respiration, and inefficient use of energy in muscles. You would give rough estimates of these as percentages, for example:

Of my 500 kilojoules of energy, if I estimate that 70 per cent is absorbed in the intestine, which is quite efficient due to its high surface area based on villi, that only 60 per cent of this energy is available to muscles, and that 50 per cent is lost as heat production as the muscles perform the work, this would leave me 500 kilojoules x 0.7 x 0.6 x 0.5 = 105,000 joules.

Experimental design

180. How can you weigh your own head?

Example answer

'If you were in 18th-century France, you could take a weighing scale and a tape measure down to the guillotines every day for a few months and collect data on the weight of heads compared to their circumference, length or any other dimensions. You would plot these data on a graph and you would be able to extrapolate an estimate of your own head based on sample data. For more accurate results, you could stratify the data by sex, age, race and alcohol use (as chronic alcohol abuse can cause cerebral atrophy), and then use a data set which more closely matches that of your profile.'

Points to note

It is unlikely that one would be able undertake this method, but this approach follows a data collection or experimental design method and shows considerable innovation. It also shows an application of your knowledge of statistics to the real world.

Alternative example answer

'You could set up a fulcrum with a plank of wood and a pivot, and lie on it in a position such that your head was on one side of the pivot, and your body on the other. You could then add weights

to the "head" side of the plank, until it balanced. At this point the moments on both sides of the plank would be equal, one side being "rest of the body", the other side being "head + weights". You could then weigh yourself, and calculate the difference in mass between the added weights and the whole body mass, giving the mass for the head.'

Points to note

This answer shows good knowledge of mechanics and mathematical ingenuity, as well as the ability to apply information that you know to a problem. Although it might not be 100 per cent accurate (the weight of the head may still be partially supported by the neck, and some of the body mass will be directly over the fulcrum and there-fore not exert a moment as its distance is zero), showing your ability to think 'outside the box' is the important point here. If you can mention these limitations in your method, this is even better.

Alternative example answer

'You could take a "bottom-up" approach by calculating the various proportions of substances within your head, and then calculate the mass of each. You could use studies from heads in post-mortems to determine the constituents of the head, for example bone, skin, hair, grey and white matter, arteries, veins, blood and connective tissue. You could then use an MRI scan to show the proportions of these materials in the head, and calculate the sum of the masses of each material. The more types of material you take into account, the more accurate the measurement will become.'

Points to note

This shows a good knowledge of anatomy and use of biological medical knowledge in the answer to the problem.

181. How could you design an experiment to find out which part of the brain controls emotions?

You could start by showing a group of people pictures showing emotional subjects, and find out which areas of the brain are active during their response. One way of doing it would be to use PET (positron emission tomography) scanning which uses radio-labelled glucose to emit signals from where it is being used. Since the brain primarily uses glucose as its energy substrate, you would tell which areas were less effective.

The importance of control groups

In this experiment, what might be the confounding factors? Since you are showing the subjects pictures in order to stimulate emotion, it might be that the area of the brain that seems active is the area responsible for, for example, vision or memory. You could try to account for this by having a control group of subjects who are also shown pictures, but rather than emotional subjects they are shown neutral pictures, such as of a football, a flower or a table. If the same areas are highlighted, then the areas affected might be accessing memory rather than emotion. You might be able to remove the effect of this by performing the experiment on subjects who are unable to access memory, for example amnesic patients.

You could also try different modalities for stimulating emotion such as auditory triggers – the voice of someone crying, for example. This might enable you to remove any confounding factors related to sensory modality.

Oxbridge interview key point

In experimental design questions, it is important that you have a test group, and that you think of a control group with which to compare, to ensure that you are getting the results you think you are. It is important to state the limitations of your study, and any weaknesses or confounding factors. Part of being a good experimental scientist is seeing where experiments might be flawed, and then coming up with solutions for them. If you enjoy this kind of activity and thought process, Oxbridge is the ideal place for you to develop these skills and apply them in cutting-edge research.

Explanation

The second type of question is the explanation type, which might be along the lines of 'Can you tell us about drowning?' These questions operate in a similar way to the guesstimate type, but in order to solve them you will use concepts from your scientific knowledge. They will require you to explain your understanding of, for example, the lung, and then extrapolate this knowledge to propose what might be happening when water enters the airways.

When answering such questions, one of the main pitfalls that students make is getting the length of answer incorrect. If you decide to ramble on for ages, you run the risk of boring your interviewers by regurgitating relatively basic information they will have heard many times that day, and this disinterest in you will be a major negative selection criteria. If you are too brief, you run the risk of not making clear links between your knowledge and the proposed explanation to the phenomenon. One of the key elements of preparation will therefore be to practise scientific explanation. Activities such as helping others with revision, and practising how to explain concepts concisely but accurately, will aid in your quest to strike a balance in terms of length.

The best way for you to improve your chances of getting into Oxbridge is not simply to learn how to answer these questions. You should come to love this type of question, and enjoy the process of stretching your mind to come up with an answer.

Oxbridge admissions tutors are looking for intellectually hungry students who are not satisfied simply by learning a syllabus.

182. Can you tell us about drowning?

Example answer

'Drowning occurs when your head is under water and therefore you are unable to breathe. The main problem is that breathing is required for the intake of oxygen for aerobic respiration and output of carbon dioxide, which is a waste product of that process. Therefore, when you are not able to make this exchange, there is insufficient oxygen. The brain is one of the most sensitive organs to lack of oxygen. Water enters the lung as the pressure inside the lungs is lower than the pressure of the water outside. This can be prevented by closing the mouth and sealing the nose, but this can only be maintained while you are conscious.

Once unconscious, you would be both unable to save yourself physically by swimming, and also unable to prevent water from entering your lungs. This would mean that you could not gain oxygen by diffusion from the air, and as more of your organs failed to receive enough, they would shut down, causing your heart to stop and you to die.'

Approach the question in a systematic way and use the chance to demonstrate your in-depth knowledge. Refer to specific processes such as aerobic respiration or ion exchange, in order to show that you can communicate comfortably with scientific terminology.

183. What medical conditions might vampires be suffering from that might explain their particular characteristics?

This question seems very difficult at first, but references to popular culture and science are becoming increasingly common and this type of question is not unheard of. The process of answering such questions should be first to consider what makes a vampire special, and then to compare these characteristics with what you know from biology and chemistry.

Example answer

'The main characteristics are that vampires drink human blood, are pale, and cannot stand sunlight, garlic or holy water. The first two characteristics may be linked, as human beings who are pale sometimes have anaemia, which is a low concentration of haemoglobin in the blood. I have seen doctors checking under the eyelid of patients to see if it is particularly white, as this is a sign of anaemia. Therefore, vampires might require a source of haemoglobin, which may come from human blood. In a hospital this is acquired by blood transfusion, which goes directly

into the veins, as it might be damaged by the acid and enzymes in the stomach. However, if vampires had an adaptation to avoid this damage, they could absorb the haemoglobin via their digestive tract, alleviating their anaemia. I can therefore speculate that their blood is being used up in some way, as they need to feed quite often.

With regards to avoiding sunlight, they could have a photosensitivity, which is one of the signs of meningitis – an infection of the layers surrounding the brain. They might alternatively have another disease, such as xeroderma pigmentosum, which vastly increases the chance of a person getting skin cancer on exposure to UV light that is present in sunlight.

The avoidance of garlic may be due to a simple allergy to a biological component of garlic. Finally, the aversion to holy water is the most difficult to explain, but it may be a confounding factor, as the water may be blessed in a metal or stone container of some kind, and therefore contain dissolved minerals that cause a reaction in a vampire.'

You may not be entirely correct, but if you can justify your answer, as well as accept criticism and learn new facts from your interviewers, you will be able to engage in an interesting interaction which will increase your chances of selection.

184. What food is best to eat before an interview?

Refer to the introduction regarding the biological metabolism of food to eat before your interview. Be sure to follow the advice given, as well as learning about the biological principles behind it!

You might also refer to the following points:

- Food that might make you ill, for example poorly cooked food, raw meat or eggs, should be avoided as they may cause a bacterial or viral gastroenteritis (infection of the digestive system).

- Alcohol should be avoided as it may slow reactions and reduce the ability to recall facts from memory.

- Supplements such as ginseng and ginko biloba (a herb) are reported to increase energy and concentration, but there is little concrete evidence to support this.

- Treatments for attention deficit disorder should theoretically increase your attention and may allow you to answer questions more precisely; however, they are prescription-only medications with serious potential side-effects, and should not be taken by non-sufferers of the disease. An example of such a drug is Ritalin.

185. When are people dead?

The simplest approach to this problem is often one taken by students. However, it can be helpful to take the process a step further back, and use the opportunity to demonstrate your understanding of human physiology. For example, even when one says that it occurs when the heart stops beating, or a person stops breathing, you may wish to comment on the fact that these processes are controlled by the brainstem, and therefore the concept of 'brainstem death' stems from this, where patients no longer have a functioning brainstem, and such functions can no longer be initiated.

There are some complications such as a deep coma or conditions requiring artificial ventilation. In this scenario, the patient is breathing, but only by virtue of a machine. Therefore are they alive, or not?

There are several other conditions where death may be confirmed, for example in massive trauma or drowning. Medically, the important parts of the examination to confirm death include the absence of heart sounds, breathing and reaction of the pupils to light.

186. Are humans still evolving?

Evolution is driven by selection pressures, which are factors that favour the survival of humans with certain traits over others. This causes the surviving humans to pass on their genes more than the non-survivors, giving rise to a change in the average genetic make-up of the population.

You may argue that many of the traditional selection pressures have been removed from the modern world. Medical technology has allowed humans with conditions that would normally prevent them from surviving to live and reproduce, and therefore the 'survival of the fittest' may no longer be playing an active role in our evolution.

However, you may argue that there is still selection going on, in terms of selection of partners for reproduction. In first-world societies, traits such as physical speed or strength are being surpassed by traits such as intellect in terms of desirability. This may be due to the fact that, on average, a higher intellect is often linked to higher earnings compared to, for example, higher strength. Therefore, the average mate might be selected in part due to the individual's earning power, giving a selection advantage to higher intellect. Further to this, people in higher socio-economic groups have a better life expectancy and therefore are more likely to pass on their genes.

In the future, you could speculate on traits that may be advantageous for selection. For example, being environmentally conscious may be favourable as fossil fuels become less readily available, and so there may be a 'green' selection pressure in the future.

Points to note

Demonstrate to the admissions tutor that you understand what is meant by evolution and try to phrase your examples with biological terminology such as 'selection pressures'. This will help the interview panel to see that your answer is directly addressing the question, even if you are being creative with your examples.

187. If you had to lose one part of the brain, what would it be and why?

This question affords you the opportunity to discuss the functions of the brain, and demonstrate your ability to discuss a relatively abstract subject intelligently.

● Sensory
  Losing one of your senses may be compared to blindness or deafness, and involves either the visual cortex or the auditory cortex.

● Motor
  Motor activity refers to activation of the muscles for all movement in the body, and is initiated by the motor cortex. Coordination of this movement is handled by the cerebellum. Losing the motor function of your brain may be similar to conditions such as motor neurone disease.

● Memory
  Memory is formed in the hippocampus, and memory loss can be either loss of short-term memories (eg being unable to retain new information), or loss of long-term memory (eg being unable to retrieve memories made in the past). This occurs in patients with amnesia.

● Emotion
  The limbic system of the brain, including structures such as the amygdala, controls mood. Disregulation of emotions or mood can occur in conditions such as bipolar disorder.

● Brain stem

This question is more open than the previous one, which is a shorter, more closed type. This allows you to discuss the concepts with a broader perspective.

Consider:

● the ability to create memories;

● the ability to coordinate movements – this facilitates participation in sports, which you may link into one of your hobbies;

- the ability to make decisions and plans – this comes from the frontal lobe, and allows you to participate in strategy-based interests such as chess, or project-based experiences.

188. How would you poison someone without being caught?

Example answer

'Owing to modern-day laboratory investigations, it is hard for me to think of a substance I could introduce into another person's body that would not be detected, apart from those that are already in there. Therefore, I might start by thinking about increasing the levels of a substance that was already present in the body, to a toxic level. I am aware that in the body potassium is involved in the conduction of nervous impulses, via the sodium-potassium pump in the membranes of cells. In the body there is a low concentration of potassium outside of the cells, and high inside. Therefore, if I inject a person with a large dose of potassium ions, by dissolving a potassium compound in water, this may interfere with nerve transmission, which may damage the brain or interfere with the contraction of the heart. I might not be suspected of foul play as potassium is a naturally occurring substance in the body. However, I would have to take pains to hide my needle mark lest I be found out.'

Points to note

This candidate uses the question to demonstrate knowledge of nerve and electrolyte physiology, and puts it to use in an evil application.

Alternative example answer

'I might try to take advantage of known side-effects of drugs that have killed people by mistake. For example, grapefruit juice affects certain enzymes in the liver that break down specific drugs. A heart medication called digoxin is one of these drugs. I could pose as a discount fruit juice salesperson, and sell the person grapefruit juice, as well as possibly mixing some into other juices I sold the person, such as orange. This would inhibit the function of the liver enzymes, allowing the drug to build up to a toxic dose and kill the person, although I have only been giving the usually non-lethal substance of a refreshing breakfast beverage.'

Points to note

This answer was impressive both in terms of its elegant delivery and cunning planning. It is limited by the fact that it only works on people taking digoxin (a treatment for the heart if it has an unusual and fast rhythm), but it shows some detailed knowledge about how the body processes drugs and is an interesting answer.

Alternative example answer

'I might use carefully planned psychological games to whittle away the person's self-esteem until other people noticed that the person was acting depressed. I could then introduce crushed paracetamol into the person's food and drink over a day, and claim that the person took an overdose of paracetamol. Practising my victim's handwriting might allow me to forge a suicide note, and I might be able ask the person to buy me some paracetamol by feigning illness and asking for help. This might cause investigators to think that the person had committed suicide.'

This is a complicated answer that shows imagination. It is thorough enough to cover several points, and demonstrates a good process to use if you are stuck, as it requires little formal knowledge (only that paracetamol can kill in overdose), but shows how you can directly answer the question in an intelligent way by structuring the answer and paying attention to detail.

189. If you were a grapefruit, would you prefer to be seedless or non-seedless?

This seems like a rather esoteric question, but allows you as a student to demonstrate the depth of your perception. The issue here is around natural selection and evolution. For the knowledge element of your answer, it is important to acknowledge the subjects. It can be helpful to think from the perspective of the object in such 'personified' questions, so that you can see what issues might affect you. Try to give a balanced answer including the advantages and disadvantages of each, as well as the limitations of your extrapolations, for example to what extent they are true.

Example answer

'As a seedless grapefruit, I would have more appeal as a product to consumers as I would be less hassle to eat. If I were a hedonist, I might choose to be a seedless grapefruit as I might get to experience more luxurious locations, such as a posh restaurant, or being made into a juice at a fancy hotel buffet. I would also be the product of genetic engineering, so I could show off to my other grapefruit peers, and I would be the "fruit" of scientific advancement. However, I would be limited to the experiences of this lifetime as I would not be able to reproduce. Since I as a grapefruit am unable to communicate, I would also be unable to pass on my thoughts, memories and memes to future generations, and I might find this existence quite empty.

If I were a pragmatist, I might wish to be non-seedless, because I would have the chance to replicate and pass on my genetic code. However, I might be condemned to a life in the shelves of a low-budget supermarket, as my appeal as a seeded fruit might be less. Also, I would probably have to die in order for my seeds to be released, so I would never see my "children" grow up.

I suppose in some ways this dilemma can be compared to couples who are choosing whether or not to have children, or looking at long-term versus short-term gains. At this point, I quite like the idea of the lifestyle of the seedless grapefruit, although this might change.'

190. Who is your favourite scientist, and why?

Example answer

'My favourite scientist is Archimedes, the ancient Greek mathematician. The Archimedes screw, the tool for raising water for which is he most famous, I actually find the least interesting achievement, as it can be considered a simple practical device of agriculture which is important but not irreplaceable by other water raising systems, most likely to be the use of slaves back in his day. The reason he is my favourite scientist is in part due to the fact that I am a keen water-skier, and as a youth, my parents would take me to various beaches around the world to let me follow my passion. I always took it for granted that I would stay afloat, but when I began to think about how it was possible, I could not explain it myself. Although I learned about the Archimedes principle that an object immersed in a fluid experiences a buoyant force that is equal in magnitude to the force of gravity on the displaced fluid, in school, I could not imagine that someone could discover this for the first time purely by his own calculations. I admire the way that his mind pursued the mathematical and scientific modelling of observations in real life. His further achievements, such as the calculation of the volume of a sphere, seem trivial but impact medical and physical sciences immensely. I hope to adopt his curiosity and scientific approach to real-life phenomenon in my future studies.'

Try not only to describe the achievements and discoveries of your nominated scientist, but also link it in with your interests.

Other scientists you may like to research include:

- Charles Darwin
- Albert Einstein
- Isaac Newton
- Nicola Tesla
- Thomas Edison
- Francis Crick and James Watson
- Leonardo Da Vinci
- Edward Jenner.

191. Can you solve this railroad problem?

Imagine you were standing by the switch of a train track that split in two further down the track. On one rail there is a child playing on the track. On the other side there are five children. You are too far away to call out or warn the children in any way, and the train is going to kill the five children on the rail, unless you pull the switch. If you do, it will only kill the one child playing by himself. What would you do?

Consider:

1 Legally, the law does not impose a duty to save the life of another person. It is therefore not a crime to let someone die, but it is a crime to kill someone. Therefore, letting the five children die is ironically legal, whereas pulling the switch and actively killing the one child may be classed as murder.

2 Ethically, under utilitarianist principles, in order to maximize the greatest good for the greatest number, you should press the switch to minimize the harm of this train accident. You may consider the quantitative nature of this problem, eg the harm to the family by means of emotional distress, is potentially five times as great if you do not pull the switch.

3 Some might argue that the role of chance or randomness is the fairest way to approach this question, as it does not involve an active selection test, which always carries the inherent risk of bias.

There is no formal 'correct' answer for this kind of problem, and it is important to substantiate your replies throughout the process.

192. If you were in charge of the NHS, would you encourage or discourage the population as a whole to have sex, and why?

This question is quite an unusual proposition, but remember to give an full account of the pros and cons of both sides before coming to your balanced conclusion.

Consider the following issues:

Pro-sex position

- More sex leads to more babies, which would eventually increase the working to non-working population and give a better economic profile to the population.

- In case of war, there would be a larger young population for conscription.

- More freely available sex may reduce the need for sex-trade workers, eg prostitution, with its associated crime and victimization of women.

Anti-sex position

- There may be an increase in sexually transmitted diseases.

- Morally, certain religious beliefs might consider this wrong, particularly if it occurred outside of marriage.

The population of the country is in decline, and there may not be a need for a 'baby boom'. If considered in the extreme, the country might not have enough resources or the infrastructure to support a huge increase in numbers, and therefore encouraging sex would be non-optional.

193. Would you argue that medicine is a science or an art, and why?

The best approach to this question is to appreciate what the sciences and arts really are.

Science

The scientific process is to establish a hypothesis, and go out to prove or disprove this hypothesis based on your findings in experiments or trials. Therefore if one were to describe medicine as processing the information from history and examination to form a hypothesis (possible diagnosis) and then going on to use blood tests, imaging and specialist tests to confirm the diagnosis (proof of hypothesis), you can see that the scientific principle is being used in each and every patient you see!

You may also refer to evidence-based medicine and clinical trials in your answer. One student brought up the fact that we may not always understand how certain medicines work, but it is usually shown that they improve certain conditions before they are used.

Art

Art encompasses the communication of feeling between humans and various mediums can be used to achieve this but in the end all art forms are about an author or artist trying to share a feeling, idea or concept with his audience. Part of the job of medicine is to cure the physical ailments of the patient. However, part of the job is to understand their suffering, how it is affecting them, their choices for treatment, and their desires for the future. Empathy helps us console relatives and patients, break bad news, and sympathize with them, and founds the basis for our motivation for care. After all, any of these conditions may one day affect us, or a loved one. Therefore medicine may be considered an art in this sense.

Avoid referring to 'instinct' in diagnosis as an art, as although this seems like an innate ability, it could be argued that this is not an instinct at all, but a quick judgement based on a vast experience base.

Summary

- The Oxbridge interview is a very different experience from a normal medical school interview and requires its own method of practice.

- Excellent scientific understanding from the school curriculum forms the basis for your approach.

- A wide reading in scientific literature compliments this.

- Practising scientific explanation, problem solving and analysis will help you to formulate succinct and informative answers.

- Almost any question can be answered using guesstimate, explanation or experimental design techniques demonstrated in this chapter.

- In experimental design answers, think about your control group and what factors you need to control for.

Appendix

List of interview questions

Chapter 3 – Motivation for medicine

Open questions

1 Why do you want to study medicine?

2 Can you tell us about yourself?

3 Can you take us through your personal statement?

4 Why do you want to be a doctor?

5 What do you want to achieve in medicine?

6 If you were to become a doctor, how would you wish your patients to describe you, and why?

Realistic ambition

7 How have you prepared to study medicine?

8 Why do you want to be a doctor, rather than enter another profession that is caring or intellectually challenging?

9 Why do you believe you have the ability to undertake the study and work involved in becoming a doctor?

10 What do you think being a doctor entails, apart from treating patients?

11 What branch of medicine do you think would interest you? Why?

12 What steps have you taken to try to find out whether you really do want to become a doctor?

13 How do you think medicine differs from other health professions?

14 How old are you when you become a consultant?

15 How long does medical training take?

16 What can you tell me about the average week of a surgeon?

17 Can you describe the average week of a doctor?

18 What would you most like us to ask you in this interview?

19 What things do you think might make people inclined to drop out of medical training?

20 Why should we pick you rather than other, better qualified candidates?

21 How might you put someone off a career in medicine?

Chapter 5 – Work experience and voluntary work

22 Can you tell me about your work experience?

23 What was the most challenging aspect of your work experience?

24 In your work experience, what skills have you learned that you can apply to medicine?

25 If you were in charge of the hospital, what would you change or do differently in terms of the ward environment?

26 What impressed you most about the doctors in your work experience?

27 Can you tell me the key things you learned from your work experience?

28 What did you learn from your voluntary work?

29 Why do people volunteer?

30 Is there such a thing as a selfless good deed; do people do things because they truly want to help others, or just to feel better about themselves?

Chapter 6 – Personal attributes

General

31 What attributes do you think a good doctor should have?

32 Can you tell me about your hobbies?

33 What are your interests?

34 What have you accomplished?

35 What would you like to change about yourself, and why?

36 What qualities do you most need to develop in yourself?

37 How do you think other people would describe you, and how would you like them to describe you?

38 Can you tell us about someone who has been a major influence on you as a person?

39 Which of your hobbies and interests do you think you will continue at university?

40 Tell us about a film you have seen or book you have read recently that has made you think. Why did it make you think?

Teamwork

41 Tell us about a time when you were part of a team. What contributions did you make to it?

42 Can you tell us about a project or group undertaking that you have been involved in?

43 Tell us about a team situation you have experienced. What did you learn about yourself and about successful teamworking?

44 When you think about yourself working as a doctor, who do you think will be the most important people in the team you will be working with?

45 Who are the important members of a multidisciplinary health care team, and why?

Leadership

46 How would you describe a good leader?

47 Are you a leader or a follower?

48 What are the advantages and disadvantages of being in a team?

49 Do teams need leaders?

Communication skills

50 Think of a situation when communication skills have been important. Can you tell us about what happened?

51 Can you learn communication skills?

52 How have you developed your communication skills?

53 What skills do you think are needed in order to communicate with your patients?

Empathy and compassion

54 What is empathy?

55 Are you a compassionate person?

Commitment and dedication

56 The study of medicine requires considerable commitment. What can you tell us about yourself that shows you have this commitment?

57 Can you give us an example of when you demonstrated dedication?

Ability to cope with stress

58 How do you cope with stress?

Honesty

59 Should a doctor be honest at all times?

Chapter 7 – Knowledge of the medical school

60 What interests you about the course at this medical school?

61 Why did you choose this medical school?

62 What do you know about the course at (... medical school) and why do you think it will suit you personally?

63 What do you know about PBL?

64 What do you think are the advantages and disadvantages of a PBL course?

65 Why do you want to come to a PBL medical school?

66 How do you study, and do you think this method will be successful at university?

67 What previous experiences have you had of learning in a small-group setting?

68 Apart from a medical education, what else will you gain from medical school?

69 How do you think you will contribute to the medical school?

70 Are there any particular hobbies or activities that you hope to pick up at university?

Chapter 8 – Medicine as a profession

71 What will be the main challenges in your work as a doctor?

72 What do you think you will be the positive aspects and the negative aspects of being a doctor?

73 Medicine involves a lifelong processes of learning, training and keeping up to date. How will you deal with these demands?

74 How will your A-levels help in your career in medicine?

75 Tell us about a scientific or medical development that has been in the news lately that you found interesting. Why has this interested you?

76 Do you read any medical publications, and if so, can you tell me about something interesting that you have read?

77 Do you read any scientific publications, and if so, can you tell me about something interesting that you have read?

78 What does being 'on call' mean?

79 What are the dangers of being a doctor?

80 How well do you cope with criticism?

81 How has information technology had an impact on the NHS?

82 Can you tell us about any significant medical stories in the media at the moment?

83 Can you tell us about something in the history of medicine that interests you?

84 What do you think is the most important advancement in the medical field in the last 100 years?

85 What do you think of the fact that nurses are now undertaking tasks that were previously done by doctors?

86 What difficulties might be faced by a person with a major physical disability pursuing a career in medicine?

Chapter 9 – Hospital life and the NHS

87 How does the hospital function at night and what problems might be encountered?

88 How do doctors relax and socialize in the hospital setting?

89 What are the origins of the NHS?

90 What does the NHS do?

91 What roles do managerial staff play in the NHS?

92 What is wrong with the NHS?

93 Who is the current minister of health?

94 Was sending men to the Moon a waste of money?

Chapter 10 – Medical knowledge

95 What is health?

96 What is the Hippocratic Oath and what does it mean to doctors nowadays?

97 How do politics influence health care provision and is this inevitable?

98 Do you think doctors should set a good example to their patients in their own lives? How or why might this be difficult?

99 In what ways do you think doctors can promote good health, other than through direct treatment of illness?

100 What is NICE?

101 What is the BMA?

102 What is the GMC?

103 What is meant by evidence-based medicine?

104 What are the arguments for and against non-essential surgery being available on the NHS?

105 What does the current government see as the national priorities in health care and do you agree with these?

106 Would you focus on preventing people from getting diseases or treating them when they are ill, and why?

107 Should doctors have a role in regulating contact sports, such as boxing?

108 Do you think doctors should ever strike?

109 How does the NHS deal with the provision of very expensive treatments for individuals, in a system of limited resources?

110 Are different social and economic groups more vulnerable to certain diseases, and if so, why and what can be done about it?

111 What are the arguments for and against people paying for their own health care as and when they need it?

112 Where does most medical treatment take place, inside or outside of hospital, and why?

113 What do you think about the way doctors are shown in the media and how do you think this will affect patients' views of their own doctors?

114 What is the biggest health-related problem in the UK?

115 Why do doctors no longer wear white coats?

116 Do you think more doctors or more nurses would be of greater benefit to the nation's health?

Important medical conditions

117 What is HIV and AIDS; how is it transmitted and how can this be reduced?

118 What is swine flu?

119 What is a pandemic?

120 What are the leading causes of death in the UK?

121 Do you think Jamie Oliver has affected the health of the nation?

122 How would you try to combat childhood obesity?

123 What do you know about asthma?

124 Explain what a stroke is. Would you be able to recognize what was happening if someone you knew had a stroke?

125 How would you know if someone you knew was having a heart attack and what would you do?

126 Should children 'play in the dirt' more?

127 What is MRSA?

128 What is *C. difficile*?

129 How are hospital-acquired infections prevented?

130 What is diabetes?

131 What signs might indicate to you that your friend might be suffering from depression and what would you do about it?

132 What is cancer?

133 What cancers do you think we can prevent?

134 Why is the HPV vaccine considered by some to be controversial?

135 What does smoking do to you?

136 What can drinking too much alcohol do to you?

137 What are the arguments for and against banning the sale of tobacco?

138 Tell us what is Herceptin is. How are very expensive treatments rationed in the UK?

Chapter 11 – Ethics and law

Consent

139 A man refuses treatment for a potentially life-threatening condition. What are the ethical issues involved?

140 The same man who has previously refused treatment for a life-threatening condition becomes unconscious. How does this change the situation?

141 Explain how organ donation is currently set up in the UK. Do you think there should be an opt-out system?

142 A male patient comes to you with flu-like symptoms two months after starting an extra-marital affair and his HIV test returns as positive. You break the news to him and explain the implications and safety issues. However, he insists that he will continue to have unprotected sex with both his mistress and his wife, who is also a patient under your care. What should you do?

143 Define medical negligence for us. Can a doctor go to jail for negligence?

Confidentiality

144 Would you prescribe the oral contraceptive pill to a 14-year-old girl who is sleeping with her boyfriend? What if her mother objected?

145 Some people feel that doctors should refuse to perform operations on obese patients. What are the issues involved?

146 Should drug companies be allowed to charge so much for their products?

147 Should drug companies be allowed to sponsor doctors' meetings and give them free products?

Resource allocation

148 Should alternative or complementary medicine be funded by the NHS, and why?

149 Should international aid organizations such as Médecins Sans Frontières (MSF) take a political stance?

150 Should the NHS fund the treatment of self-inflicted diseases?

151 Should we treat patients for emphysema or heart disease who continue to smoke?

152 Suggest how funding health care using a system based on health insurance might be better than the NHS. What would be the problems?

153 What would be the benefits of legalizing currently illegal drugs and what would be the pitfalls?

Abortion

154 What is the law regarding abortion in the UK?

155 Would you perform abortions as a doctor?

Fertility

156 Explain what human rights are. What human rights do you know and how are they enforced?

157 What are the issues involved in in-vitro fertilization?

End of life issues

158 What is your feeling about euthanasia?

Medical research

159 Should animal testing be used in medical research?

160 Trials of new medications involve risk to the health of individuals and can result in serious injury or death. How can we justify this?

Child issues

161 If you were the doctor working in accident and emergency, and a parent brought in a child with burn marks that looked suspiciously like cigarette burns, what should you do?

162 Should people be allowed to sell one of their kidneys if they wish?

Chapter 12 – International students

163 How do you feel about the prospect of studying in the UK?

164 Can you give any examples that demonstrate your independence?

165 What are the differences in health care between the NHS and the system in (your home country)?

166 How will you cope with being away from your support networks?

167 What difficulties do you think are faced by students studying in a language that is not their first language?

Chapter 13 – Graduate students

168 How will your degree be useful to you in your career in medicine?

169 What made you decide to switch career paths?

170 Do you have any teaching experience?

171 Do you have any experience with research that you can tell us about?

172 Why did you not choose to study medicine as an undergraduate?

Chapter 14 – Oxbridge

173 Why are you applying to Oxford (or Cambridge)?

174 Why are you applying to this college?

'Guesstimate'

175 How many footballs can you fit into an aeroplane?

176 How much water is there in a horse?

177 How many animals did Noah take on the Ark?

178 Is hell exothermic or endothermic?

179 How high can I climb having eaten only a banana?

Experimental design

180 How can you weigh your own head?

181 How could you design an experiment to find out which part of the brain controls emotions?

Explanation

182 Can you tell us about drowning?

183 What medical conditions might vampires be suffering from that might explain their particular characteristics?

184 What food is best to eat before an interview?

185 When are people dead?

186 Are humans still evolving?

187 If you had to lose one part of the brain, what would it be and why?

188 How would you poison someone without being caught?

189 If you were a grapefruit, would you prefer to be seedless or non-seedless?

190 Who is your favourite scientist, and why?

191 Can you solve this railroad problem? Imagine you were standing by the switch of a train track that split in two further down the track. On one rail there is a child playing on the track. On the other side there are five children. You are too far away to call out or warn the children in any way, and the train is going to kill the five children on the rail, unless you pull the switch. If you do, it will only kill the one child playing by himself. What would you do?

192 If you were in charge of the NHS, would you encourage or discourage the population as a whole to have sex, and why?

193 Would you argue that medicine is a science or an art, and why?